S0-ARB-379

# CONTEMPORARY MORAL ISSUES
## Facing the Orthodox Christian

# Stanley S. Harakas

*Originally published as "Contemporary Issues."*
*Newly revised and expanded.*

Light and Life Publishing Company
Minneapolis, Minnesota
1982

Light and Life Publishing Company
P.O. Box 26421
Minneapolis, Minnesota 55426-0421

Copyright © 1982
Stanley S. Harakas
Library of Congress Catalog Card No. 81-83927

All rights reserved. No part of this book may be reproduced, stored in a
retrieval system, or transmitted, in any form or by any means, electronic, mechanical, photocopying, recording or otherwise, without the
written permission of Light and Life Publishing Company.

ISBN 0-937032-24-7

*"To (God) be the glory for ever and ever. Amen" (2 Timothy 4:18).*
*And*
*In memory of my father, Samuel S. Harakas*
*1898-1981*

# Contents

# Contents

## PART III SEX AND FAMILY ISSUES

## PART IV SOCIAL ISSUES

# INTRODUCTION

This volume is a revised and expanded edition of a book originally published by the Greek Orthodox Archdiocese Press, entitled *Contemporary Issues: Orthodox Christian Perspectives*. The source for the majority of the contributions to this volume (as well as the previous edition) was the column "Exetastes" which appeared in the *Orthodox Observer*, the bi-weekly newspaper of the Greek Orthodox Archdiocese of North and South America. In addition, a number of articles have been included here, written for another purpose. Some of the original articles have been substituted by these newer offerings and others from the original have been dropped since they dealt with concerns no longer of relevance. In all, the number of topics has been increased from thirty-eight to forty-seven. The original division has been retained: Faith Issues, Church Life Issues, Sex and Family Issues, and Social Issues. The articles have been lightly revised and edited, chiefly with the purpose of making them more applicable to the present day. But, in general they have retained their orignal tone and character. Retained, as well, is the basic approach to these topics. The topics discussed deal with some of the vital issues which concern Orthodox Christians as members of local parishes, dioceses and the national Church. The topics concern us as well in our capacity as citizens, and as persons faced with many social, political, economic, medical, moral, cultural and religious issues. The effort, in the pages which follow, is to view these issues from a concretely Orthodox Christian perspective.

Many of the resources drawn upon are specifically based on the Greek Orthodox Archdiocese of North and South America Clergy Laity Congress Social and Moral Issue, decisions. But it is felt that most of these Archdiocese quotations are representative of a general Orthodox consciousness. More fundamentally, the Bible, the Holy Tradition of the Orthodox Church, our Theology and that indefinable, yet quite real and powerful "Spirit of Orthodoxy" are the guides used to address the various questions discussed. The major concern in dealing with some of these modern and heretofore barely addressed issues will be their religious, spiritual and ethical dimensions. They seek to shed light not so much for a theoretical perspective, but rather for the practical life of Orthodox Christians seeking to respond to contemporary dilemmas in a genuinely Orthodox Christian way. This book seeks to discover and examine the spiritual and moral dimensions of these problems, guided always by the light of faith, the beliefs and the traditions of the Orthodox Church.

This last statement will cause the careful reader some thoughtful reflection. The Orthodox Church has no ready formulae and pat answers for many of the contemporary problems which we face in our modern techonological society. The best which can be done at this time is for some Orthodox Christians living today to seek to examine, test and evaluate these new and challenging questions of our time from the perspective of the Orthodox worldview. That is what I have sought to do in these pages. Consequently, this means that what you read in these pages is not the infallible voice of the Orthodox Church on all the topics discussed. Rather, what you will be reading is the product and the conclusions of one person who has some knowledge of the Bible, Holy Tradition and the doctrines of the Orthodox Church, and who has some familiarity with how Orthodoxy has approached similar problems and issues in the past. In many cases, as the text makes clear, the tradition of the Church's teaching is quite firm and unambiguous. However, in others, the positions presented are the author's effort to understand these new issues with what he feels would be the "mind of the Church," a not unrisky business.

Consequently, this book exists to stimulate the reader to approach contemporary issues from the perspective and viewpoint of the Orthodox Christian Faith. With that ground rule clear, it is possible that you will disagree with what you read here. In that case, several things may be happening. You may not be making your judgments from basically Orthodox Christian standards and are reflecting prejudices, philosophies or religious teachings alien to Orthodoxy. On the other hand, you may be simply misunderstanding what has been written. However, you may have well understood, and disagree with my conclusions and views, based on your own understanding of the Orthodox Christian tradition. It is hoped that when this occurs, it will become the occasion of fruitful discussion and clarification of the issues until an Orthodox consensus can be formed. Thus, especially in the cases of new and unaddressed issues, dialogue and discussion will take place, so that finally, the Church as a whole will decide through its synodal system and provide an official directive to the faithful. Till then, may these little essays serve to promote some reflection and serve, as well, as guidelines for living as Orthodox Christians in an increasingly complex world, filled with moral dilemmas for the Christian conscience.

A quick glance at the table of contents will assure the reader that the topics treated do not exhaust the issues which could have been dealt with. However, there are enough of these issues covered to provide a useful beginning. It should be noted that as newspaper articles and as position paper drafts prepared for consideration by semi-official church bodies, they neither exhaust all of the dimensions of the topics discussed, nor do they strive for theological and academic comprehensiveness. They do, however, seek to speak not to the specialist, but to the concerned Christian of today, as he or she sits in the pew, lives in the home, labors in the working place, and exercises the duties of the citizen.

The author and the publisher hope that these offerings will be used in the Church by pastors, camp counselors, religious education directors, and teachers to help make Orthodoxy more relevant to the daily lives of our people.

I wish to express my special thanks to Light and Life Publishing Co. for issuing this new and expanded version of the original book. Thanks too, are accorded to Mr. Takis Gazouleas of the Greek Orthodox Archdiocese Press, Inc., for turning over to me the publication rights of the original book. I am also very grateful to His Eminence Archbishop Iakovos who granted permission to me to use some of the position papers originally produced at His Eminence's direction for use by the Social and Moral Issues Committee of the Clergy-Laity Congress, held in Atlanta, Ga., in 1980. Mention needs to be made as well of my students in numerous courses who stimulated my thinking on many issues and who demanded, frequently, to know "the Orthodox position" on these and many other issues. I wish, especially to acknowledge the substantial help of two students who, under my direction, wrote the first drafts of several of the included position papers. They are Christopher Bender, who served as my teaching assistant for a number of years, and Diane Leonidas. Many thanks, as well, to my wife, Emily, who assisted in the typing of many of the articles when they originally appeared in the *Orthodox Observer* and to Cathy Lazarides who typed the position papers between the assignments she had for me during my last year as dean at Holy Cross Greek Orthodox School of Theology.

Finally, a word of thanks to Dr. Thomas C. Lelon and the board of trustees of Hellenic College and Holy Cross Greek Orthodox School of Theology who, upon my request, relieved me of administrative duties so that I could return full-time to my teaching and writing responsibilities, one small fruit of which has been the preparation of this present volume.

August 3, 1981
Feast of Isaacios,
Dalmatios and Faustos,
the Righteous
Brookline, Mass.

# Part I

# FAITH ISSUES

# 1. WHAT IS ORTHODOXY ALL ABOUT?

Among those of us who take the role of the Orthodox Church seriously in our lives, there is oftentimes expressed a confusion about what is really at the heart of our Faith. Some emphasize the dogmas; others, the canons. Others see worship at the center of Orthodoxy, and for some it is tradition, usually understood in some single aspect of it—music, iconography, architecture, monasticism, etc.

What is Orthodoxy all about? Well, even as we try to answer the question, we should be clear that no really complete and total answer can be given to such a question. We can, however, clarify some aspects of the issue.

## Orthodoxia

Our faith is *Orthodox* in two different, yet interrelated ways. Our "Orthodoxia" is first of all a "correct belief." The word "orthon" in Greek, means correct, or right. "Doxa" has two meanings, the first of which is "belief." The Orthodox Christian Church holds that it has maintained the original, true and correct understanding of the teachings of Christ and the Apostles for the twenty centuries of its existence. To be "Orthodox" is to share in that unchanged affirmation of the truths about God, the world, man, salvation, the church and what is to come in the future.

But "Orthodox" has another meaning, too. The Greek word "doxa" also means praise or worship. Our Church sees itself as the "true worshipping Church." These two meanings of "doxa" are clearly interrelated. True worship and true faith of necessity intermingle and enrich each other. A person who is truly an Orthodox Christian knows that faith without expression in worship is dead. And conversely, worship without faith is equally dead. The Lord taught that we are to worship in spirit and in truth. "God is spirit, and those who worship Him, must worship in spirit and truth" (John 4:24).

### Orthopraxia

Another dimension of our Orthodox Christian Faith is *orthopraxia*. The word "praxis" means to "act" or "action." The Orthodox Faith is not just the affirmation of belief, nor is it only participation in the worship of the Church. It is also the living of the Faith in our lives. It applies first of all to us as individuals as we seek to cultivate the inner life: prayer, self-discipline, fasting, patience, purity, etc. Its second application is in our interpersonal relations; the chief dimension of Orthodox Christian orthopraxia is agape-love. Learning to concern ourselves and to act on behalf of our neighbor's well-being, without selfish interest, is the main task of orthopraxia. This has special meaning as it is applied to our fellow Christians, to those of the "household of the faith" (Galatians 6:10). Its final application is concern for the well-being of our society: its political, economic and social life, especially as these influence the lives of the poor, weak, unprotected and disadvantaged people of our cities and towns and countryside.

### Orthokoinonia

But Orthodox Faith, Orthodox Worship and Orthodox Ethics do not exhaust the meaning of Orthodoxy. We can coin a word to describe this next aspect of Orthodox Christianity: *"Orthokoinonia."*

Orthokoinonia means true community living, with special reference to the local parish. Truly blessed and happy is that Orthodox parish where the majority of the members put Christ first and at the head of their parish life; where the most meaningful social event in the lives of the Christians takes place on Sunday mornings in the temple; where the main task of the parish is encouraging learning and service in the name of God; where there is little conflict, jealousy, gossip and selfishness manifested among the members; where mutual concern, cooperativeness, humility, patience and interest in learning about the Faith are exhibited; and where—above all—love is chief. Such a parish is truly worthy of the title "Orthodox Christian Community."

### Orthokrisia

Finally, *orthokrisia* is a mark of the Orthodox Christian Faith. It means "correct judgment." In fact, it means keeping our values in place. Orthodoxy sees spiritual things as the most important aspects of human living. Other concerns are important, of course. Health, both physical and mental; material goods; the body; education; honor; respect; achievement in all fields of human endeavor; all these and more are important. But Orthodox Christianity sees all of these things subject to a higher criterion: the criterion of the Spirit. Orthodox Christian living subjects all things in life to that criterion. All values in life are finally ranked by their relationship to God, His will for us, and our growth as persons and as a people in His image and likeness.

Orthodox Faith, Orthodox Worship, Orthopraxia, Orthokoinonia and Orthokrisia serve as markers for answering the question "What is Orthodoxy All About?" But within these boundaries there is tremendous freedom of behavior and style of life. From the orthodox monk in a Mount Athos skete, to the Orthodox housewife Sunday school teacher, to the Orthodox student in a secular university, to the Orthodox executive in a modern American corporation, and in hundreds of other situations, Orthodoxy is lived and practiced as a way of life. This combination of

Orthodox specifics and Orthodox freedom is what Orthodoxy is all about.

## 2. CHRISTIANITY AND EASTERN RELIGIONS

During the past decade and a half an increasing number of young people—and not so young people—have become interested in eastern religions. This interest is quite widespread and goes much beyond mere intellectual curiosity. Not a few young men and women raised in the Orthodox Church have been attracted to such religious views. Some have made a sharp break with the faith of their fathers. Others have become selective in their emphasis and have sought to combine their allegiance to Orthodoxy with their newly found convictions. Others live a "split-personality" religious life: functioning as Orthodox Christians on Sundays and holy days and reverting to another conviction on other days.

### The Reasons
Many analysts of our age have sought to explain this turn of many youth to the Far East for religious inspiration. Curiosity, going along with the crowd, rebellion against authority, the generation gap, the shrinking world and many other plausible reasons are given. But most of these reasons can also be used to explain the drug culture, alcoholism in youth, the so-called sexual revolution, political extremism of both the right and left, and the new attitudes of youth toward higher education. Certainly they all play their part. But a closer analysis of the common emphasis of eastern religions points to a more significant and profound reason.

### The Common Emphasis
Anyone who has tried to understand eastern religions is

quickly impressed by the amazing diversity. Uninformed people often look at Christianity and deploring its divisions, point to other religions as examples of unity and cooperation. The facts, however, are quite different. For example, Hinduism is divided into three major "ways" with substantially different outlooks on life and fundamentally varied religious practices. And, even within these basic "ways" of Hinduism, there are thousands of modes of devotion and religious practice, all of which are tolerated, if not approved by the adherents of that religion. Buddhism, too, has its varieties of belief. Hinayana Buddhism, "the lesser vehicle" as it is known, has many expressions. However, Mahayana Buddhism, "the greater vehicle" has many, many more. An examination of Taoism, Confucianism, Shintoism and the myriad of combinations which exist convince one of the bewildering variety of eastern religions.

Yet, there is also a common thread which rests at the core of most expressions of eastern religions. It has a positive and a negative aspect. Positively, there is an emphasis on the oneness of all being. Accordingly, for eastern religions distinctions, separatedness, divisions are illusion. Ultimate reality is one. Thus, it is possible to emphasize our human unity with nature, with each other and with ultimate reality. For people rebelling against individualism, against the competitiveness of modern economic life, against racism, against the inhumanity of the industrial and technological society, it seems made to order.

The negative aspect of this view must also be noted. It follows that if "all is one," the most basic division affirmed by Christianity—the distinction between God as creator and everything else as creation or creature—must be denied. And that is what in the final analysis all eastern religions do: they deny the existence of a living, personal, creating, saving, sanctifying God who is ultimately different from the created world, even though He be closely related with it.

## Their Appeal

The appeal of these eastern religions rests primarily in the fact that they are religious without believing in God, as he is understood in the West. Rather than being an escape from the impersonal, patterned, orgainized life of the western world, eastern religions basically reflect that life! The final consequence of eastern religions is that personhood, individuality, interpersonal relationships, including ethical distinctions, are all considered to be illusory and nonexistent. Without realizing it, by rejecting God, the drive for more naturalness, more humanity, more interpersonal warmth is finally denied.

Orthodox Christianity, more than the churches of the west, has always begun its understanding of the nature of God by pointing to the Trinity of God. Though God is radically different from His creation, He also sets the pattern for His creatures in His own being. God is Trinity. Three *persons*, Father, Son and Holy Spirit, are in continual and eternal interpersonal relationship. The creation in its present condition tends to move toward the impersonal, the mechanical, the patterned. When human beings fully identify with creation as it presently is, they lose their identity as human beings. Only when we become God-like, when we communicate with the ultimate reality who is a *trinity of persons in community* can we achieve the real balance of existence for which most people strive: individual worth relating to others in community.

Those who rebel against the evils of the western world, "throw out the baby with the bath water" when they reject Christianity, especially, Orthodox Christianity. The real rejection is the rejection of God. To reject God is to invite not only self-delusion but also to reject unity with Him who is truly "ultimate."

## 3. THE DEVIL, DEMONS AND THE EXORCIST

The film "The Exorcist" and its sequel together with

the many films regarding evil powers have proven to be of great interest to the movie-going public. In his review of "The Exorcist," an Orthodox columnist recommended the picture, but also suggested that some Orthodox writer provide information on the subject of Exorcism for the faithful. What follows is a brief explanation from the Orthodox perspective.

In the films and in occult literature, demon possession is presented as an unusual, readily identifiable phenomenon which causes the possessed person to act in fearful and paradoxical ways. It is presented as a terrifying and rare experience. The exorcist faces the demonic reality in a dramatic face to face personal encounter. He exorcises the devil, that is, in the name of God he commands the devil to depart from the possessed person. There are at least four things which need to be said about this phenomenon: the reality of the devil and demons; the meaning of demonic possession; who are exorcists; and the value of movies such as "The Exorcist."

## Are Devils and Demons Real?

While to raise such a question 200 years ago would have been ludicrous, today it is a fair and honest question. One or two generations of liberal education has lumped "devil talk" together with all sorts of chicanery, superstition, fortune-telling and astrological nonsense. In the past, perceptive people knew that "devil talk" was much more than that. Essentially it spoke of a deep and disturbing reality—the reality of evil in our lives. Some intelligent people, however, separated what they called the mere "personification" of evil as the devil and demons, from the "reality" of evil. By doing this, evil became just a concept—an idea to be included in systems of philosophical and theological thought. Interesting, but powerless.

Only when it became respectable in recent years to understand that symbols and symbolic language made truth an existential reality in the lives of people, did the ancient practice of identifying evil with the devil begin to make profound sense to earth-bound minds. The Church has always taught the reality of the devil and his angels—the demons—as powerful adversaries both of God and His people. In his fascinating book, *The Screwtape Letters*, the famous author C. S. Lewis argues in his delightful "correspondence" that the devil's biggest weapon against humanity is a disbelief in him. Those who are able to identify the devil as a personal enemy are one step ahead in the struggle against evil.

But even those who are still uncomfortable with such an understanding can fully comprehend how "devil talk" makes real the power and insidious influence of evil in our lives. Whether you say "the devil," or simply leave off the "d", the fact remains that the fundamental reality is the same.

### What Is Demonic Possession?

"The Exorcist" and much of the contemporary discussion makes the tremendous error of seeing (the d)evil's work as an unique and terrifying phenomenon only *occasionally* experienced. The Gospels, of course, do present demon possession as an object of Jesus' healing work. But both the Bible and the Church understand (the d)evil's pervasive power as much more common, much more widespread, much more a part of our lives than "The Exorcist" type of experience implies. It is (the d)evil at work in us when we lie, steal and commit adultery. It is (the d)evil at work in our society when radical injustice triumphs; when poverty flourishes amid affluence; when thousands of lives are daily aborted before they are born. It is (the d)evil at work when nations prepare for "peace" with multiple overkill atomic weapons, germ warfare and genocidal policies.

The Scriptures speak of the "Prince of this world" and the dragon "who makes war . . . on those who keep the commandments of God." We pray daily ". . . and lead us not into temptation, but deliver us from evil (or, just as correctly, 'deliver us from the Evil One')." The world, in large part, is possessed by (the d)evil. It is a daily experience, lived from minute to minute.

## Who Are Exorcists?

Exorcism means to banish (the d)evil from our lives. *Exorizo* means to put someone "beyond the boundary," that is, to banish or exile. Religiously and spiritually, this is applied to (the d)evil. *Christ is the chief exorcist.* His death and resurrection were His initial victory over (the d)evil. He is *Christus Victor.* "Iesous Christos Nika" ("Jesus Christ is Victorious") say the ancient inscriptions. He is victorious over (the d)evil.

*The Priests are exorcists.* When they baptize, when they confirm, when they hear confession, when they conduct the Divine Liturgy, when they preach the Word of God, (the d)evil flees and the grace of God abounds.

*Every Orthodox Christian is an exorcist.* As he or she struggles against personal sins, fights against immorality in family, neighborhood, state and nation, it is a battle against the Prince of this world, (the d)evil.

The whole church, past, present and future, has the task of an exorcist: to banish sin, evil, injustice, spiritual death, the devil from the life of humanity!

## What Value "The Exorcist"?

Films such as "The Exorcist" are useful because they draw the attention of many to this dimension of reality which we would prefer not to contemplate and not to comprehend. Many have seen these films merely as entertainment and have been amused. Some have seen them only to become physically nauseated or shocked by the technical virtuosity of the film's directors and actors. Others viewed the films from morbid curiousity. None of these is central to a Christian evaluation of these films.

Whether we see it or not, the real message for us is this: the adversary of God and goodness and true human life is real. He is the enemy and we must contend with him until he is defeated.

## 4. ASTROLOGY AND OUR FAITH

One of the most characteristic things happening today in our country is the revival of all sort of views and approaches to life which had at one time been dismissed as "unscientific foolishness." All of us have noted a wide spread increase in astrology and various forms of occultism, such as satanism, witchcraft, spiritism, etc.

### The Christian Presuppositions

As Orthodox Christians we may respond to this sort of development in one of three ways, at least. We can see it as a positive sign that people are searching for reality which goes beyond the mere physical; or we can see it as an indifferent phenomenon of little or not interest or regard to us; or we can see this development as a threat to the Orthodox Faith, a denial of the Christ-like way of living, and a destructive way of believing, thinking and acting.

In order to arrive at one of these conclusions it is necessary to ask ourselves what the Orthodox Faith teaches about God and man's nature, then see how it fits the views which make up the astrology and occult movements.

If you think about your Orthodox Faith for a moment, you will note that as Orthodox Christians we hold that God is creator and ruler of the Universe and all that is in it. The familiar icon of the "Pantokrator" found in the domes of our Orthodox churches is a reminder and expression of that great truth of our Faith. It is the belief of Orthodox Christians that "ours is our Father's world" and that our trust and hope and dependence is ultimately upon Him alone.

Our Orthodox Christian view of man notes that people are both sinners and weak, yet also potentially God's image and His likeness. The difference is dependent upon our relationship with God. And *that* is dependent upon our willingness to choose *for* God or to *deny* Him. Orthodox Christians hold to the belief that man is free to make this choice.

Now, if we look at these two beliefs (that God is master of the world, and that we are, however, free to choose either for or against Him) then we will see very easily what our attitude ought to be when we compare this Christian belief with astrology and occultism.

### Astrology

Astrology is an attempt to describe the future of an individual, based on the position of certain stars relative to the period of the year when that person was born. Astrologers make calculations on this basis and predict what events, happenings and opportunities may occur in the life of that person. People may read an astrological prediction for the price of a newspaper, have a chart prepared by an astrologer for substantially more money, and now, even have an astrological reading prepared by a computer.

At the basis of this astrological prediction-making are two very interesting presuppositions. The first is that the position of the stars at birth control the destiny of every person born on earth. The relationship of those physical bodies determines what kind of personality I have, what will happen to me, how my life shall be lived.

The other presupposition is that men and women are subject to this accident of birth for their whole lives; a person cannot escape from the determining influences which arise from the fact that he or she is an Aries or a Sagittarius. In the view of astrology, we are not really free to choose and develop our own destiny. We are forever subject to the blind and mechanical influences arising from the physical location of the stars at the time of our birth!

## A Conclusion About Astrology

It is not difficult to determine what an Orthodox Christian view about astrology will be. In effect, astrology denies the loving and gracious Lordship of God. It replaces God with a mechanical view of the determination of the future by the stars. In the place of the glorious freedom of man presented to us in the Christian Faith, it describes a star-haunted mankind, forseeing the inexorable influence of the stars on his life, as he squirms and struggles to escape the inevitable.

Astrology both denies the kingship of our loving and gracious Heavenly Father, and the glory as well as the responsibility of our own freedom. Even though astrology pretends to point to what is presented to be a force beyond mere materialism, it does no such thing. It is a denial of the fundamental truths of the Christian Faith.

As such we cannot be indifferent to it, nor should Christians share in it or encourage others to share in it. Horoscopes in newspapers should be ignored as denials of the love of God and man's moral and spiritual freedom! Christians should persuade other Christians not to have anything to do with astrology. Of the three options mentioned above, astrology is definitely a denial of the Christ-like way of living; something to be rejected as unchristian!

## 5. THE OCCULT AND CHRISTIAN LIFE

Though the occult has many different forms, its dominant characteristic is its identification with and friendly attitude toward evil. There is a qualitative difference between a naive consultation of astrology charts and the invocation of the devil to accomplish one's purpose. While astrology is simply a denial of two of the fundamental truths of the Christian Faith the occult is a positive identification with the forces of evil.

## The Occult and Christ

The occult, at heart, is identification with *evil*, and the use of the power of *evil* to obtain one's desires, purposes or goals. Known as Satanism and devil worship, it is obvious that the whole ethos of the Church is designed to resist such identification with the forces of darkness. The most famous confrontation between Godliness and devil worship is described in the Gospel of Matthew during the forty day period that Jesus fasted in the wilderness (4:1-17). There the message is made very clear:

> *Once again, the devil took him to a very high mountain, and showed him all the kingdoms of the world in their glory. "All these," he said, "I will give you, if you will only fall down and do me homage." But Jesus said, "Begone, Satan! Scripture says, "You shall do homage to the Lord your God and worship him alone" (Matthew 4:8-10).*

In another place in the same Gospel, Jesus was charged that he healed people through the power of the devil: "It is only by Beelzebub, prince of devils, that this man drives the devils out" (Matthew 12:24). In response Jesus drew the line between His goodness and that of the evil embodied in the devil, when He stated:

> *Every kingdom divided against itself goes to ruin; and no town, no household, that is divided against itself can stand, And if it is Satan who casts out Satan, Satan is divided against himself; how then can his kingdom stand? And, if it is by Beelzebub that I cast out devils, by whom do your own people drive them out? If this is your argument, they themselves will refute you. But if it is by the Spirit of God that I drive out the devils, then be sure the kingdom of God has already come upon you (Matthew 12:25-28).*

## The Occult and The Church

The church's continuation of the work of Christ as the Kingdom of God, the Kingdom of Light, the salvation of men from evil and of Christ's victory over death, sin and evil, clearly make it violently and sharply opposed to all forms of occultism. We see this in the theology of the Church, which explains the saving work of our Lord Jesus Christ as victory over the force of evil in the life of mankind. The exorcisms of the baptismal service and the joy of the midnight Resurrection service point to this fundamental enmity between the church and any movement which would identify itself with the powers of evil. In the words of the Apostle John, "the Son of God appeared for the very purpose of undoing the devil's work" (1 John 3:8).

## The Occult and the Christian

There are many of us who find it hard to believe in a personal force of evil, Satan or the devil. Though the Church has taught the existence of a personal devil from its very beginning, the one very clear and obvious thing to even the most sophisticated of us, is that the power and force of evil is very real. From "sophistication," many who have denied both God and the devil have now fallen into the service of evil and submitted themselves to its power. Some of these have "rediscovered" the devil and turned to Satanism and devil worhsip. A recent issue of a national news magazine highlighted the resurgence of occultism in our cultivated, highly educated and technological society. It is a sad commentary on our secular society, which seeks to push out the influence of Christian faith from its public life, for in the place of the religion of Christ, there now appear the covens of superstition and devil worship.

As a result, Christians are unalterably opposed to all forms of occultism, with special avoidance of those forms which direct themselves overtly into any kind of relationship with *evil*, regardless of the name given it.

Long ago the New Testament book of 1 Peter gave the necessary direction to all Christians:

> *Awake! be on the alert! Your enemy the devil, like a roaring lion, prowls round looking for someone to devour. Stand up to him, firm in faith . . . and the God of grace, who called you into his eternal glory in Christ, will . . . restore, establish, and strengthen you on a firm foundation. He holds dominion for ever and ever. Amen. (1 Peter 5:8-11)*

## 6. EVOLUTION: A HERESY?

Recently the issue of Evolution has become a topic of public discussion. Many people are heard arguing against the theory of evolution, and specifically the teaching of it in the public schools. In some states in our country, there has been an effort to remove any kind of teaching about evolution from public school textbooks, or at least permit or require the teaching of other views. Some very sincere and dedicated Orthodox people have joined those forces in the name of Orthodox Christianity. For them, the teaching that living forms have evolved over the years in their development is a denial of Christian truth and therefore is a heresy. Is evolution a heresy?

### Fact

Evolution, first of all, must be recognized as being two things: a fact and a theory. The fact consists of the readily identifiable truth that various groups of living beings have actually gone through changes with the passage of time so that descendants of original forms differ from their ancestors. To deny that fact would be to fly into the face of all of the evidence gathered painstakingly from all over the world by anthropologists and paleontologists. For example, anthropologists have traced the development of the horse from an early dog-sized creature, to the contemporary large-sized animal. They have also discovered the remains of various forms of mankind and dated them by scientific methods. There is no denying the *fact* of some kind of development, some kind of evolution.

### Theory

However, evolution is more than just these gathered facts. It is also a theory. Rather, to be more accurate, there are many theories of evolution. Theories serve as attempts to explain the facts in a coherent and rational way. It is in the area of "theory" that the popular idea of evolution as having an "ape for an ancestor" developed.

Few people realize that many efforts have been made to interpret the fact of evolution. Numerous theories are purely materialistic. They hold that man's development was an accident and occurred by happenstance, according to materialistic laws which function independently of any cause or purpose. Other theorists find this highly improbable. They hold that the evolution of man could not "just happen." They calculate that the mathematical probabilities of such a sustained accident taking place are infinitesimal. According to these theorists, it takes much more to believe that the human race is an accident than it does to accept the hypothesis that there is a goal and a purpose toward which the evolution moves. Two such theorists are Le Compte du Nouy and Tielhard de Chardin.

### The Difference

In his book on evolution, the well-known Orthodox theologian, Panagiotis Trempelas, points both to the *fact* of evolution, as well as to the various *theories* of evolution. The first cannot be denied. However, there is a world of difference among the various theories. Some of those theories are definitely heretical. Not because they hold that evolution has taken place, but because they deny any place in their interpretation of the facts of evolution for the spiritual dimension of the reality of existence.

Other theories are closer to Christian truth. In posting a "telos" or goal, in rejecting a purely mechanical interpretation of evolution, these theories are more congenial to the spiritual verities of the Christian Faith. Thus, Trempelas concludes: ". . . it appears more glorious and divine-like and more in harmoney with the regular method of God, which we daily see expressed in nature, to have created the various forms by evolutionary methods, Himself remaining the first and supreme cause of the secondary and immediate causes to which are owed the development of the variety of species."

Recognizing the difference between facts and theories which explain the facts, it is necessary also to note that as long as Christians recognize the creative power of God in the process of evolution, it is both bold and hasty to call evolution a heresy.

## 7. THR CHARISMATIC MOVEMENT

Perhaps the most controversial movement to touch the Orthodox Churches of our country during the past few years has been the "Charismatic Movement." The proponents of the movement are touched by deep experiences which are attributed to the Holy Spirit: speaking in tongues, joyful praise of God, the sense of salvation. It is these gifts which cause the participants to be called "charismatics" ("charismata" means "gifts" in Greek).

### Good or Bad?
A number of years ago the Orthodox College Fellowship held a seminar on the topic. They noted many positive results from involvement in the Orthodox Charismatic movement. In their judgment, the positive points include the

following: a call for genuine renewal; actual renewal for some Orthodox Christians; a call for an ongoing conscious Christian life; study of holy scripture; renewed devotion to the sacraments of the church; renewed interest in the life of private and corporate prayer.

The conference seminar on the Charismatic Movement also noted what it called "weak points." These were: excessive individualism; exaggerated emotionalism; self-righteous elitism; alarming relativism of doctrine; overemphasis of such spiritual gifts as "tongue-speaking"; and, disturbing dependence on group psychology and psychic techniques.

Others have been much more critical. In a pamphlet entitled *The Pentecostals,* published by a Chicago group associated with the promulgation of the writings of Apostolos Makrakis, Chrysostomos Stratman writes, "It would be a great mistake to look to the Pentecostals and other 'charismatic' exponents of instant, painless mysticism for inspiration, example or guidance. To do so, is not only illogical and anti-orthodox, but completely vain and futile."

The general stance of the Church, however, seems to be found somewhere in the middle. As long as the movement encourages the life of faith, and especially sacramental participation, prayer, bible study and identification with the Orthodox Christian spiritual life and heritage, many church leaders see a positive advantage to it. Insomuch as the Orthodox charismatic movement is divisive and tends toward the formation of "conventicles," threatening the Church with schism and heresy, it will continue to be looked upon with suspicion by the Church at large.

## Positive Approaches

Since then traditional Orthodox and "charismatic" Orthodox have learned something from each other. What have traditional orthodox learned from the charismatics?

They have learned that the Orthodox Christian Faith can be a joyful, feeling and involving experience. Too many of our parishioners attend their local church with a "club mentality." The more serious Orthodox are often ponderously serious. The scriptures are too full of the feelings of joy and happiness as it relates to the Christian life to justify making a virtue out of moroseness. Charismatics have taught conventional Orthodox Christians that their emotions belong in the Faith, together with customary behavior and their intellect. Enthusiasm for prayers, telling other people about the faith, expecting God's presence in daily life, looking to the Bible and spiritual writings to be guided and inspired: these are all pluses for the traditional Orthodox Christian as he or she draws from the experience of the Orthodox charismatics.

But charismatics have also learned some lessons. The Orthodox Christian Faith is the jewel of our Church. Its balance, wholeness, inclusiveness and due consideration for the totality of revelation is now more respected. Those who ignored it, soon became extremists who ended up being committed to one heresy or another. Private truths and private visions are subject to the judgment of the Church as a whole. There is virtue in quiet piety; there is spiritual growth which takes much effort and years of suffering to mature; there is faith which cannot be articulated always; there is Christ-like *agape* which doesn't always have the aura of religiosity; there is the Orthodoxy of the altar and the chalice which can never find a substitute; and, there is the unity of the Church which must never be broken.

### Good Sense

Much good sense has characterized the relationship of the official Church and the Orthodox charismatics. Much of the charismatic movement within the Orthodox Church in this country is of God, and the Church has found much good in it. For example, the Greek Orthodox Archdiocese sponsored three national "Orthodox Spiritual Life and Renewal Conferences," as a result. Those aspects which were a faddish reflection of a similar phenomena on the American scene, have lost their appeal and will disappear in time. Thus charismatics kept in touch with the real life, faith and communion of the "Mother Church." And the Orthodox Church in America was challenged to focus on its spiritual life in these difficult and trying days. For both, St. Paul's ancient words of wisdom continue to apply:

*". . . discern the will of God, and . . . know what is good, acceptable and perfect" (Romans 12:2).*

*"Do not stifle inspiration, and do not despise prophetic utterances, but bring them all to the test and then keep what is good in them and avoid the bad of whatever kind" (1 Thessalonians 5:19-22).*

*"Be alert, stand firm in the faith; be valiant and strong. Let all you do be done in love" (1 Corinthians 16:13-14).*

# Part II

# CHURCH LIFE ISSUES

## 8. ECUMENICAL DISCUSSION ON CHURCH SUCCESS

Several years ago, in the National Council of Churches' newsletter, the president of the National Council of Churches offered a book review of Dean Kelly's book *Why Conservative Churches Are Growing.* In the interchange between these two NCC personages, there is something for Orthodox Christians to learn.

In her review, Mrs. Cynthia C. Wedel, NCC president, noted the thesis of the Kelly book is that conservative churches among the various protestant bodies had been gaining members at a very rapid rate. The reason given for this great growth is that in a time when so much about our society takes away meaning and significance from life, the fundamentalist and conservative protestant churches manage to provide it for increasing numbers of persons. However, in the view of Kelly, these churches provide meaning in life for their adherents "by making strict demands upon their members and fostering a sense of unity which punishes deviation from group norms."

Mrs. Wedel, a liberal protestant, was not too happy with this legalistic approach. She sees it as a challenge to "those of us who value individual freedom, variety and tolerance in our religious institutions." Her problem is whether it is possible to provide this sense of meaning, belonging and purpose for life, without having to impose rigid membership qualifications and exclusive criteria of belonging.

Her response is of real interest to Orthodox Christians. "The clue which the book gives is that we must find ways to bring people into a rediscovery of the age-old and basic meanings of the Christian faith. These represent the true 'conservatism' of the church." However, Mrs. Wedel persists in turning the "basic meanings of the Christian faith" into a "liberating and revolutionary gospel" without defining what that means.

## Lessons For Orthodox Christians

This description of the ends of the protestant spectrum is highly enlightening to the Orthodox Christian who would examine his own Church in terms of providing meaning and significance for life. Dean Kelly points to the fact that the conservative protestant groups are growing because they impose demands upon their faithful and require performance and not just lip-service. Mrs. Wedel sees this as a rigid legalism and counter-proposes the age-old faith and teachings of the Christian message as the real giver of meaning. She recognizes that the liberal protestants have not led their people to that age-old faith, but rather, have "substituted semi-secular types of fellowship for the intense encounter of small groups of Christians struggling to understand the meaning of faith for their own lives."

What does this mean for Orthodox Christians? First, there is a comforting observation to be made. When we look at the Orthodox Faith and teaching as it has been lived throughout the centuries we see that the extreme positions of legalism on the one hand and social revolution on the other have both been avoided. Our Orthodox Faith has managed to keep in balance both concerns.

The Orthodox Faith *does* make demands upon the faithful. It is clear that being Orthodox means the acceptance of the faith of the creeds, the councils and the fathers of the church. It means respect for the canons of the church, the rules and regulations of the Christ-like life. Yet, the Orthodox Church has always tempered its concern for rules with grace and "economy." Orthodoxy is not a legalistic faith. On the other hand, the Orthodox Church has always felt a concern for the world in which it lived. The well-known patristic synthesis with its re-interpretation of Greek thought, as well as the development of early Christian philanthropy and concern for social improvement, point to that aspect of the faith. But, above all, Orthodoxy has pointed to the need for men and women to love God and to commune with Christ. Knowing who God is; that He sent His Only-begotten Son into the world for our salvation; that the church continues the work of forgiveness, sanctification and theosis; that faith, worship and deed are inseparable: these make up the essence of Orthodoxy. This concern with the purity of the faith keeps orthodoxy from degenerating to legalism or transforming itself into warmed-over religiously tinted political activism.

## Challenge to the Orthodox

This book review provides a challenge to all Orthodox Christians that we not be tempted to follow either one of the two protestant extremes in our own day. Some Orthodox have already turned Orthodoxy into their own peculiar brand of legalistic Orthodox fundamentalism. Other Orthodox have turned the church community into an ethnic social club, with little regard for the content of the faith and the sacramental, ethical and spiritual life inherent in Orthodoxy. The challenge to us is that we live the Orthodox Faith in its true spirit: that the Orthodox Faith be at the center of our lives, pointing us to the true life in the Father, the Son and the Holy Spirit. The rules will then have their legitimate place; the genuine spirit of Christian social concern will also be expressed; worship will be real and moving; and the fruits of the Spirit will grow among us. The challenge to us is not to deviate from—but to hold onto the "age-old and basic meanings of the Christian faith"—genuine and true Orthodox Christianity!

## 9. ECCLESIASTICAL CRITICISM

In the middle of the eighteen hundreds a new style of religious literature came into existence in Greece. It can be called "journalistic ecclesiastical criticism." Its main purpose was to ferret out wrong-doings by the hierarchy, to publicize the wrong-doings, and, hopefully, to thus improve the life of the church. The first practitioner was a man by the name of Apostolos Makrakis.

Many people followed his footsteps. Greece is full of small organizations, even today, whose purpose is to cultivate their own piety and their own understanding of Orthodoxy, as well as to take verbal pot-shots at the ecclesiastical establishment. Not so long ago, the United States was treated with the establishment of the first newspaper/magazine whose major purpose seemed to be related directly to this tradition.

Now, we must all admit that there is a certain satisfaction in criticizing our superiors. There is even more satisfaction in reading the criticism of church leaders who are supposed to be above criticism. That's what makes such columns so juicily interesting. Of course, reading such magazines in order to receive some vicarious thrill from "this month's attack" has little to do with the development of Christian character. Love doesn't enjoy the evil that others do (1 Cor. 13:6).

### The Good of It

But is it really all bad? No, it is not. This kind of reporting serves a very important purpose in the life of the church. It would be a sad day for the church if there was no voice of criticism. Even though it always runs the danger of being self-serving and personally aggrandizing for its own sake, journalistic ecclesiastical criticism is valuable.

First, journalistic ecclesiastical criticism prevents

bishops, priests and layleaders from acquiring the impression that they can act, decide, function and speak as if they were responsible to no one. It is very much within the spirit of the Orthodox Church's teaching about the church to give a place for expression to the whole church; to the lower clergy, to the monastics, to the laity. In America, our government is structured so that there is a system of "checks and balances." In some small measure, journalistic ecclesiastical criticism serves the same purpose. No actions, whether official, or private and personal (if that is possible for churchmen), thus escape notice and comment. It is one of the many ways which the church used to monitor its own behavior.

There is another reason why journalistic criticism in the church is valuable. It helps raise and examine some of the issues of the life of the church. Recently, the language question, the role of Hellenism in Orthodoxy, the Americanization of Orthodoxy, jurisdictional issues and other such topics have received some public airing because the various segments of the Greek Orthodox press have criticized, evaluated and judged official and unofficial actions and statements of church leaders and representatives.

## The Bad of It

For these two reasons journalistic ecclesiastical criticism is both useful and helpful in the ongoing life of the Church. But criticism is a very dangerous practice for the Christian. Jesus warned "Judge not that ye may not be judged" (Matthew 7). The churchman or layman who undertakes the criticism of his fellows, opens himself to the same kind of critique and should be careful, as St. Paul admonishes, that he who would teach others does not himself fall.

But there is an even more pernicious consequence waiting in the wings for the professional critic. And that is to use criticism of others for personal promotion and for the projection of an unseemly "holier than thou" attitude. The critic's criticism may well not only harm his own spiritual growth, but also his exclusive critical bias may turn others into bitter, negative, depressed and depressing devotees of a negative piety. Criticism tears down. There is the danger that criticism will do only that. And "the building up of the church" becomes its first victim. It is only with the deepest fear of God and the most sensitive caution that criticism should be practiced.

The final danger is related to the virtue of criticism, in that it helps raise and clarify the issues. The danger is the great temptation to switch from the issues to personal invective; from the general judgment to personal attack. The suspicion is raised that this happens when the arguments are weak regarding the issues. What begins as high-minded concern for the welfare of the church degenerates into unchristian, unbrotherly and unspiritual personal malice.

### With Great Fear

It is with great fear and trepidation that a churchman—clergyman or lay-person—should raise the banner of criticism, as necessary as it is. Journalistic ecclesiastical criticism is not inviolate—it, too, is subject to criticism!

## 10. A LITURGICAL SUSPICION

In the past I have had a suspicion. A liturgical suspicion. And it is this: that very few Greek Orthodox Christians really utter any conscious prayer when they attend the Divine Liturgy! I based this suspicion on the following observations.

### External Behavior

The first is the external behavior of most of the Greek Orthodox faithful in our churches today. Let's start with choir members, who, one would suppose, do more praying during the Divine Liturgy than any person other than the priest. Yet, from watching both directors and members, the concern which is evident is not the meaning of the words they sing, but the kind of music and its performance which counts. The end product of their efforts seems to be musical tones, not consciously experienced hymns of praise and glory for God. But at least there is some sort of activity in the choir loft!

The external behavior of most of the church attendees gives very little evidence of any internal spiritual behavior at all. Most Orthodox Christians come late. I remember an old priest who told me one time that he counted the people who were in church during the epistle reading, and then doubled it in order to know how many people would be in church that day.

The majority of the adults stand poker-faced and stiff for the whole service. Many never make the sign of the cross. Numerous worshippers show absolutely no response when the priest censes them or blesses them. In those churches where service books are placed in the pews for the congregation to hold, the larger proportion of them rest unopened in their slots. In those parishes where the people are led in singing of the hymns, or repeating the Lord's Prayer and the Creed, what is heard generally is a loud whisper, rather than a vigorous response of a people eager to express their prayers aloud.

### Why Go to Church?

A second reason which makes me suspect that very little conscious prayer takes place during the Divine Liturgy most of the time, in most of our Greek Orthodox Churches, is the variety of reasons people give for going to church. Now, I am sure, no one expects that all people would go to church for the same reasons. Or for that matter, that the same person would go to church every Sunday for the same reason. The most popular reasons for going to church, however, which I have heard, do not include prayer. "A good example for the children," is probably the most popular reason. Other explanations frequently heard are: "It is necessary in order to keep the traditions alive;" "The sermon is the most important thing for me;" "I like the music;" "It is the only place I can go together with my whole family on a regular basis;" "The priest is a swell fellow;" "I go to church out of habit;" "It's so restful;" "It's a good show!" But never, or hardly ever, "So I can pray, so that I can be with the other people of God, communicating in the depths of my heart with my Lord and God."

So I have a suspicion—a liturgical suspicion. I suspect that most Greek Orthodox Christians never say a single, conscious, heartfelt prayer when they attend the Divine Liturgy! They may "get into a religious mood" and may "feel good" from the sense of duty done, but my guess is that they never talk to God, personally, individually and consciously.

(This article, when originally published provoked a number of responses. The next chapter describes some of them.)


## 11. RESPONSES TO A LITURGICAL SUSPICION

In response to the view that very little, if any conscious prayer took place during the Divine Liturgy in most of our churches there were many varying and different answers written to this author.

On the one hand, a substantial percentage of those who wrote agreed with the general position. A response from the southwestern part of the nation said in part: "Your suspicion about lack of true prayer and true involvement in the Liturgy is a *fact* . . . and I sincerely feel that there must be some changes in the Liturgy, some simplifications, and more of the Liturgy spoken in English . . . People don't involve themselves because to many of them it is a performance, a *great traditional performance* with elegant robes and *unnecessary* repetitions."

Another respondent, also from the southwest wrote: "I would like to state here that the Liturgy lasts too long. . . . The congregation should take part in the singing. . . . By singing all together, one becomes conscious of what he sings, and that is good for the soul."

One writer from up-state New York feels that the blame is not only on the individual churchgoer: "The church cannot absolve itself from its failure to inspire people to attend services . . . What is probably most revolting is the 'country club' type atmosphere adopted by many parishes. . . . Indeed, one attending services today receives the impression of a paid admission type of performance. The problem of church attitude is a cancer that will be painful to overcome."

A California writer pinpointed his agreement with the "Liturgical Suspicion" by pointing to "women who talk while the service is going on" and speaking of the choir as "a continuous lullaby. No distinction of word. Much discord."

A woman who is not an Orthodox, but married to an Orthodox man pointed to "a lack of desire to attend services. I believe that the true reason is that most of the people do not have a personal relationship with Jesus Christ. If they did, then their daily life would be led by the Holy Spirit, and joining together with others of like minds would be eagerly looked forward to as a time of fellowship in which to praise the Lord together."

Some others, however, acknowledged some elements of truth in the suspicion, but proceeded to give evidence in the other direction through their personal testimony. A New Yorker began with "Three cheers to you, and also my hat goes off to you. You have put into words what I, too, have suspected through the years." This writer however, in speaking of her own personal experience, wrote these moving words: "I, personally, must talk and pray to my God when I am in church. There are so many things I ask him to help me with that no other person could ever do for me. Because he is a God of Love, I know my many prayers and questions will be answered." This writer also disagreed with the view that the choir did not really participate.

Another writer from western Pennsylvania agreed that "most Orthodox Christians do not participate during the Divine Liturgy." This respondent then proceeded to tell of her own experience. "For quite awhile I was completely unaware of what goes on during the Liturgy. . . . During the early years of my life I had little need of God and less need for the 'hypocrites' who attended His churches. Then came a period of searching. I thank God that after visiting many churches, He led me to (this Church). The first Sunday I attended Liturgy, I was overwhelmed by the presence of God's Spirit. The grace of his gift touched my heart and opened my mind to reveal to me the mystery of this truly Divine Liturgy. . . . I must say, yes, I pray at each Liturgy." And she tells of praying "that each church will be blessed in the near future with the overwhelming power of God's Spirit" as her church has been.

Another writer, from the West, agreed that "I never did pray and my mind was miles away. Church was something I felt was a social obligation. You notice all of this was in the past. Since our Lord, Jesus Christ, has become very personal to me, I look forward to Sundays with great anticipation . . . The Lord is with me at all times, but when I enter His house it's magnified. I don't miss a Sunday (because I enjoy it so). I love to sing and do so in the congregation where I sit. When I am not singing, believe me most of the time I am praying silently."

Others took me to task as being quite wrong. A Minnesota Orthodox wrote these words of reassurance: ". . . one of the main reasons that I attend the Greek Orthodox Liturgy on Sundays is so I can pray . . . I also sing in the choir, which is my main joy, and it is a form of continuous prayer . . . I also do know that all members of our prayer groups definitely go to church mainly to *pray*."

An Orthodox Christian from Missouri expressed great opposition to this view, refuting it point by point and concluding with an exhortation to humility on the part of your author.

Was the "Liturgical Suspicion" justified? In part, yes. But we also saw that many of our faithful Orthodox Christians definitely "Get Much Out of Going to the Liturgy." Do you?

## 12. WHAT ARE PARISH COUNCILS FOR?

There is an amazing variety of answers given to our title question. Parish council members have different views, priests disagree among themselves, the laypeople have their own judgments, the archdiocese takes another perspective.

### Some Opinions

A large percentage of *parish council* members think of the council as one would think of the Board of a large commercial corporation. Membership on the council for them smacks of the "captains of industry" feeling. Some other parish council members see the council as "the local ecclesiastical employer" whose function it is to hire and fire a range of personnel, including priests, assistant priests, janitors, secretaries, afternoon school teachers, etc.

Some *priests*, however, are convinced that parish councils exist for the sake of making their lives miserable. They would be pleased to have them disappear from the scene. For other priests, the council provides an instant circle of friends, possible "koumbari" and readily available golf partners. Many priests, more practically, tend to view the council as a glorified finance committee to be used to raise money for the church.

Many *laypeople,* viewing the parish council from the outside, tend to see it as a sort of civic service, much the same as the local United Fund committee, or Kiwanis club. For others, the council serves as a first step to elected office, or as a platform for public exposure, an ego builder whose purpose is to project personalities.

Finally, for the *archdiocese,* the parish council's function is often seen as purely administrative. "Article V, Parish Administration" of the *Uniform Parish Regulations,* states, "Each parish shall be administered by the priest and a Parish Council cooperatively." As defined elsewhere in the *Regulations,* most of their duties have to do with financial management (Article XIII, Duties of Parish Council).

## A Theological Understanding

As we look at all these varying understandings of the purpose of the parish council, we can agree that in them there is some value. For example, even the view that the council serves to project attention on some of the parish members has a measure of truth, for are we not taught by the Bible to "honor those to whom honor is due?"

However, there is another understanding of the purpose of the council, based on our Orthodox understanding of the church. Two aspects of that teaching are important for a theological understanding of the role of the council.

First, it is our Orthodox teaching that the church continues the work of Christ on earth. Some of the things which the church does in order to fulfill its task include continuing the teaching word of Christ; mediating His saving, forgiving and strengthening grace to the world through the sacraments; maintaining the community of the "people of God" in this world; pronouncing the will of God for mankind; directing the spiritual life of the believers, etc. The local church is as much responsible for these tasks as are patriarchs, archbishops and synods, for the local church is where the church *really is!*

## Clergy and Laity

That points to the second aspect of the Orthodox teaching about the church, which helps us understand the purpose of the parish council. The church, it is taught, is made up of all those who are baptized, live the sacramental life and accept the Orthodox truth. The important thing to see, is that this means that the church is made up not of clergy alone, but of the clergy and people together. But if that is true, then it must also be true that *both the clergy and the laity together do the work of the church!* Naturally, that includes *all the laity*. When laypeople sing in the choir, teach Sunday school, instruct their children to pray, etc., they are doing the work of the church. In a more organized way, parish councils concentrate the efforts and the participation of laypeople in doing the work of the church.

Parish councils help do the work of the church. And "the work of the church" is to continue the work of Jesus Christ in the world. The council is one of the ways the laity of the Orthodox Church share in the church's work of preaching, teaching, blessing, sanctifying, directing, guiding and realizing the community of believers. The council is not *just* a finance committee. It is not *just* an administrative device. It is not *just* an aid to the priest. It is not *just* an ecclesiastical employment office. It is all of these things and more. But they all make sense when they are seen as necessary aspects of doing the Lord's work. Thus, when the Parish regulations of the Greek Orthodox Archdiocese were revised in 1978, a spiritual dimension was given to the description of their duties: "The Parish Council under the leadership of the Priest shall have the following

duties: to attend divine services regularly, and to participate in the sacramental life of the Church thereby setting
an example for the Parish, to administer the affairs of the
Parish in such a manner as to aid the Priest in the fulfillment of its aims and purposes . . . ."

When a parish council member undertakes his duties,
he takes an oath of office before the priest and the people.
In part, he says "I will uphold the dogma, teaching, traditions, holy canons, worship and moral principles of the
Greek Orthodox Church . . ." He does this as a baptized,
communicating, faithful and obedient member of the
Church of Christ. As a council member, he undertakes an
important share of the church task to continue the work of
Christ in and for the world. What does a parish council do?
It helps continue the saving work of Jesus Christ. And that
is probably the most important thing you can say about a
parish council.

## 13. TEACHING RELIGION

Can it be done? Some seriously question if it is possible
to teach religion! That may seem a strange and irrelevant
problem for you—unless, of course you care about the future of the church. The problem is that religious education
in our churches is not always successful. At the heart of
that failure is a basic and fundamental mistake about the
teaching of religion.

### Religious Education in the Past

How many middle-aged American born Orthodox
Christians complain bitterly about the lack of Sunday
Schools and an organized religious education program during their childhood days! They feel that they were cheated
and sometimes hearken back to some local situation which

formed the exception to the rule. "But," they say, "thank God, we now have a Sunday school program which educates the young people in our Faith." These Orthodox Christians love their church and their children. They assume because a Sunday school has been organized, literature provided, a schedule devised, and a teacher positioned at the head of the class, that religion is being taught to the church of the future.

## Today's Religious Education

In our own times, we have built on that view of religious education. Most parish leaders have complaints about our religious education efforts, pointing to the need for better-trained teachers, improved materials and strengthened national leadership. Because we have some shortcomings in these areas, we feel that the solution to our problems about "teaching religion" is more of the same.

Yet, if we are honest with ourselves, we would admit that our religious education efforts have not succeeded in "teaching religion" very well. We see our teenagers, the products of our organized religious education effort, bored with the church—uninterested, uninvolved, eager to escape from the church! We have bred a generation of non-church attending youth who have gone through our Sunday schools and are now only peripherally involved in parish life. We have not taught them how to live religiously. We *have*, however, had some success in teaching them *about* religion! We have informed a goodly number of young Orthodox Christians *about* the Faith, the history of the church, the sacraments, etc. But the numbers of young Orthodox Christians who are characterized by zeal and enthusiasm for the church is small. The Orthodox youth (and their elders, too) of our day are not generally marked by enthusiastic love for God. Eager experience of the life of prayer, study of God's Word, decision-making in the light of the Gospel, full and conscious involvement in the liturgical life of our church, are not the most dominant notes of our parish life!

Somehow, we are not managing to "teach religion;" that is, to communicate to our youth and others the excitement, commitment, zeal, faith, hope, and love of the Christian Faith. We are filling minds with facts—but we are not moving hearts and wills!

### People Catch Religion

The fact is that religion cannot be taught in the classroom. Orthodox Christianity, especially, is a way of life, a mental set, a spiritual perspective. It involves love for God, and man, and sacramental living. It requires faithful and self-sacrificing commitment. But these are just words if they are not experienced!

We, the maturer Orthodox Christians in America, deceive ourselves badly if we think that "religious education" is brought about primarily by classrooms, religious texts, and elaborate Sunday school schedules. People "catch" religion, they are not instructed into it. When religion is experienced in an atmosphere alive with faith, devotion, integrity and love, *then* religion is taught!

This is not an appeal to close Sunday schools. Nor in any way should it be construed as an attempt to weaken agitation for more and better teaching materials. Budgets for Sunday schools and religious education must be increased.

But let us not deceive ourselves. Only the living faith of the local Church can provide the experience that "teaches religion," that truly communicates Faith and makes it live in the hearts of youth. Religious education stands or falls primarily with what goes on in the Orthodox Christian home, at the Divine Liturgy, at the hospital bedside, in the prayer life of the believers and on the level of the interpersonal relations of Orthodox Christians in the world. Formal instruction *about* the Faith builds on that experience—it can't create it!

## 14. MASONRY AND THE CHURCH

Of special interest to Greek Orthodox Christians in the United States is the relationship of the Orthodox Church with Masonry. Many Greek Orthodox men are Masons and share actively in the life of the church. They have heard of changes and criticisms directed against Masonry, and cannot understand why such attacks should be made by some people in the name of the church, since "like the church, Masonry teaches we should believe in God." Others, however, continue to teach that Masonry is "the great enemy of Christianity," and "allegiance to Masonry is denial of the church." What are the facts?

### A Little History

Though some historians of Masonry trace its history to Lameck, the architect of the Temple of Solomon in Jerusalem, and others to Zoroaster, Confucius and Pythagoras, it appears that Masonry has its historic beginnings in the guilds of masons and builders of Medieval Europe. These very powerful "unions," little by little, became clubs with a political character, especially in England.

At first, they were strongly Roman Catholic in membership. Through political influence and the support of the Stuart line of English Kings, they later took on a protestant character. Finally, they became what might be called "theoretical Masons," which had nothing to do either with builders or politics. They became a secret society, with teachings, temples and rituals, which were unique to themselves.

On June 24, 1717 the "Great Lodge of England" was established. It became the "mother Lodge" for all of worldwide Masonry. The main lines of Masonic ritual were set down by one James Anderson, a protestant clergyman, and accepted by the Great Lodge in 1723.

Masonry spread to other countries, arriving in Massachusetts in 1735. Because it was protestant in character, the Roman Catholic Church soon expressed strong disapproval of the movement. Pope Pius VII in his encyclical of 1821, *Ecclesiam a Jesu Christo*, condemned and rejected Masonry. Also, the Holy Synod of the Orthodox Church of Greece, following the advice of a pan-orthodox conference held in June, 1930, on Mount Athos, also condemned Masonry.

## The Teachings of Masonry

What has caused this criticism of Masonry? Of course, the political question is no longer an issue. The crux of the matter is the message, or basic teachings of Masonry. As we noted above, the first Masons were Roman Catholics. The guilds insisted that members be faithful Roman Catholics. When Masonry became predominantly protestant, its teachings were already fundamental Christian teachings. Anderson taught, originally, that Masons should follow the religion of the State (in the case of England at that time: protestantism in its Anglican form). Shortly afterwards, however, this began to change. A broad humanistic type of religious teaching supplanted it. In some forms of Masonry, such as French, Latin and Greek Masonry, the teachings became very rationalistic, anti-Church and secular.

In English and American Masonry, a broad, diluted, general kind of religious teaching became the norm. Thus, in Masonic teaching, all religions are on the same level. Their differences are attributed to various levels of cultural development, reflecting an evolutionary development toward an understanding of some broad and general truths about some supreme "Great Architect of the Universe." Through the rituals and teachings of Masonry, the individual Mason may select and cultivate for himself the broad and general truths of ethics and religion. While referring to God, and having the Bible placed on the altar of the temple, Masonry neither imposes a specific understanding of God, nor does it require a Mason to accept the Bible and its teachings as the revealed Word of God.

## The Church's Response

Though the Church accepts that there are some broad and general truths of ethics and religion to be found in all Faiths and in all places, it cannot accept such a teaching as the final word. Since the church points to Jesus Christ as the Savior of the world, and to the sacramental life of the church as the means by which man is redeemed and sanctified, it must criticize those who would reject that affirmation, as teaching "less than the whole truth." The serious danger is that persons will become content with some general and philosophical idea of God, and forget that "God so loved the world that He gave His only-begotten Son that whosoever believeth in him shall not perish but have everlasting life" (John 3:16).

## A Word to Masons

The question ultimately boils down to what Christ, the sacramental life and the Orthodox Church mean to you. You may know of some Orthodox Christians who have become members of Masonry, and who have taken from it many things which have strengthened their faith. They feel that their present involvement in the sacramental and community life of the Church has been strengthened by their participation in Masonry.

However, you may also know of many Orthodox men who have become so identified with the life, the ritual, the social connections and teachings of Masonry that it serves as a real substitute in their lives for Christ and the Orthodox Church. To these latter Masons, I would say that the caution and criticism of the church is justified. To the first, Orthodoxy must raise the serious question of ultimate loyalty to Christ and the Church. That the danger is there; it cannot be denied. That the difference in teaching is real, cannot be denied. That identification with un-Orthodox Christian ritual has drawn many of the faithful away from the life of the church, cannot be denied. That it does not have to be this way, also, cannot be denied!

Orthodox Christian! Where do your loyalties rest? That is the question the church would have *you* answer in the discussion of "Masonry and the Church!"

## 15. WOMEN IN THE CHURCH

A frequently asked question is "What is the place of women in the Orthodox Church?" It reflects the increasing sense of openness regarding the place of women in our public, economic and social life. A number of protestant churches have permitted the ordination of women. Even the Jews have seen the first woman Rabbi undertake pastoral responsibilities. In many ways, the various religious groups are reflecting the social changes of our times. Looking toward the future of Orthodoxy, as well as to her past, how do we as Orthodox Christians see the role of women in the church?

### The Church's Perspective

The most important fact we have to note is that the church's interest in every situation is different from the views of the "world." The church's major concerns are the redemption and salvation of people, without reference to gender. St. Paul put it best when he wrote that in Christ "there is no male or female." Further, the church knows that all of her members are both equal and different. They are equal before God's judgment, mercy, grace and love. St. Paul notes that "God is no respecter of persons," that is, God doesn't play favorites. But just as there are varying functions in every organized body, so it is in the body of the church. In the church, each individual functions most appropriately when the purposes of salvation, spiritual growth, the worship of God and Christian love are fulfilled by and for the whole community of believers.

Throughout the centuries the church has found that the cultivation of faith among the young, and the support of the moral life of the mature, as well as the spiritual direction of all the faithful together with the improvement of society in general, have taken place best with the assignment of concrete roles to the sexes. Generally speaking, men have been given the public aspects of the Christian life for their concern, and women have been responsible for the private sphere in the life of the Christian community. The priesthood, for instance, had been reserved for males. But everyone knows that the important "church in the home"—to use St. Paul's phrase—receives its most significant leadership from its female members.

The church knows full well that should the family cease to do its work for the Christian nurture of children, for the cultivation of Christian attitudes toward all the major issues of life, and in the personal relationships of the members, then "the public church" faces hard and difficult times.

### The New Age

As we've noted above, the church's past experience has made this division of labor into an effective and successful way of realizing its goals. In a new age, with the new circumstances which surround us, it may be that the church will change. On the other hand, the only reason acceptable for that change would have to be the improvement of the Christian life. Right now, most arguments about new roles for men and women do not appear to contribute to the growth of faith, the increase of Christian community, or the salvation of souls. Theologically speaking, a strong case can be made for the ordination of women in the Orthodox

Church. Though, of course, an equally strong argument exists for the other side. That really is not the issue. The issue is: are people being helped to become Christ-like?

## An Important Position

Right now, the place of women in the church can be seen in an important four point "job description." Women, above all, are believers and baptized members of the body of Christ. Their personal task is the cultivation of the spiritual life. Together with all Christians they seek to realize in their own lives the power and saving grace of God. Second, women are laypersons. The vast majority of men in the church are laypersons, too. Laypersons share in the task of continuing the work of Christ. Thus, when women help in the conduct of worship, live the prayer-life and assist at the sacraments, they help do the work of the church. When women teach in the home and in the church school, and when they point to Christ's lordship in the community and the home they help continue the work of Christ.

Third, women reign over the "church in the home." The Bible has a remarkable phrase, indicating that "through childbearing, women shall be saved." Whatever else this verse may mean, it points to a most important role in the life of the church for women. Finally, even though the public role of women in the church will probably increase in the future, the long standing influence of Christain women on men—especially husbands and sons—will not decrease, in all likelihood. Long ago, St. John Chrysostom pointed to the beneficial influence of Christian women on men.

In conclusion, as long as women continue to love Christ, practice the life of prayer, participate in the sacramental life, and continue to exemplify the Christian virtues of love, mercy, faith, gentleness, forgiveness, patience, and goodwill, their place of importance in the church will remain secure.

## 16. GAMBLING, MONEY AND THE CHURCH

One of the dominant themes in the report of the Clergy-Laity Congress of 1974 was opposition to gambling as a means for raising funds in our Greek Orthodox parishes. For a small number of priests and laypersons, who for years had been fighting a lonely and unsupported battle against gambling in our parishes, it was a welcome, if surprising development. This prohibition was subsequently repeated in other Clergy-Laity Congresses of the Greek Orthodox Archdiocese, as well as by other Orthodox jurisdictions in the United States.

But for many parish leaders, clergy and lay alike, the decisions against gambling practices for the purpose of raising funds for parishes, parochial schools and other parish and archdiocese activities, are threatening.

### The Case for Gambling

These leaders are concerned because they know that the financial stability of their parishes, schools and other projects—for which they have labored so long and hard— may be endangered by the anti-gambling decisions of the Congress. They ususally defend parish gambling practices on reasons drawn from experience, and not ideologically.

Few will argue that gambling is a fine and noble practice, replete with Christian values, an aspect of the gospel which should be increased and practiced widely for its own intrinsic good. The proponents of parish fundraising through gambling say that in the past our people did not learn to give to their church freely as a grateful response for God's many blessings. Consequently, the necessary funds had to be enticed from the members in other ways for value received. Hence, rigid assessments, legally imposed in the form of dues; "church" dances held to assist in meeting the budget; bake sales and bazaars; and, of course, gambling practices (usually raffles, but as of late, elaborate "Las Vegas Nights" have become the vogue in some areas of the country).

Financial difficulties have pushed parish leaders to an even greater reliance on gambling in order to balance their budgets. They argue: "Since our people don't give freely and generously without some form of enticement and since more and more people are 'too busy' to help in projects, such as bazaars, bake sales and car washes, we are forced to turn to gambling as a last resort." Though it is not easy to sell raffle tickets (it takes time; it obligates the seller; and sometimes it invites rebuff and embarrassment), the appeal of "windfall winnings" and "something for nothing" returns a good profit for the time, energy and money invested. In short, it works.

For the supporters of these practices, the future doesn't look much different from the past or the present. Basing themselves on a low estimate of the faithfuls' ability or willingness to change, they project that "the people aren't interested in re-orienting their giving practices. They'll never be motivated to the point of giving to the church for spiritual reasons. All you will do is lose valuable income, wreck the stability of our parish institutions, and, finally, fail to change human nature which jumps at the chance to participate in the excitement of winning big prizes for a small wager."

## A Look at the Arguments

If the above is a fair description of the proponents position, then there is something to be grateful for: there is no feeling for gambling as a positive good, as something to be promoted for its own sake. That means that if some other, equally effective means were to be found and implemented, there would be no acceptable reason to continue parish gambling practices.

Further, we must agree that historically, gambling was

introduced because our people had not learned to give to the Lord's work for spiritual reasons. In the villages, from which the majority of the first immigrants came, both church and school were supported by state funds. Church giving was in the "nickels and dimes" category for candles and priestly beneficences. The situation in the immigrant communities was quite different. The funds required were substantial and were needed on a regular basis. Our people and their parish councils entered into a not-so-honorable game: "We-give-as-little-as-we-can; You-figure-out-pain-less-ways-to-pay-the-bills" was its name.

But the present situation is not so uniform as it was in the past. In many parishes that game is no longer acceptable. Priests and parishioners are becoming convinced that the financial dimension of our parish life is an integral part of the religious dimension. They have read the scriptures and heard St. Paul say:

> *He who sows sparingly will also reap sparingly, and he who sows bountifully will also reap bountifully. Each one must do as he has made up his mind, not reluctantly or under compulsion, for God loves a cheerful giver. And God is able to provide you with every blessing in abundance, so that you may provide in abundance for every good work ... You will be enriched in every way for great generosity ... for the rendering of this service not only supplies the wants of the saints but also overflows in many thanksgivings to God ... Thanks be to God for this inexpressable gift! (2 Corinthians 9:6-15).*

The willingness of many parish leaders to accept the basic principles behind the Fair Share Program and the increasing number of Greek Orthodox laypeople who enthusiastically support the philosophy of giving articulated by the League of Greek Orthodox Stewards (LOGOS) fundraising approach, indicate a changing attitude today. We cannot accept that the "dues system" is received with the same equanimity as it was in past decades. This is, however, only a trend. It is found mostly in the medium-sized parishes. But things are changing!

What the future will be like depends a great deal on the church's spiritual leadership. The Archbishop has taken his stand on the side of a more Christian approach to giving. If bishops and priests follow his lead there is no reason to remain pessimistic about the future. Change to more spiritual giving patterns on the part of our people will take time, but a church which teaches the transfiguring power of the grace of God cannot consistently assume a "they'll never change" attitude about the future.

### What's Wrong with Gambling?

The reason most arguments against gambling as a church fundraising method have been largely ineffective is that they are not appropriate to the parish situation. Gambling is condemned usually as a destructive passion ("Gamblers Anonymous"), as taking bread from the hungry mouths of deprived dependents, and as an expression of a greedy attitude. The fact that most parishes must "push" their raffle tickets with the appeal "Help the Church" makes those kinds of arguments (valid in different situations) unconvincing in the parish setting.

We have not read our New Testament carefully enough. The work of the church has always needed money. And the church has always had to receive its support from the donations of the faithful. And Christians have always felt it was a part of our Christian calling to give for the work of the Lord. Because all that we have is held in trust by us for God, the Christian is a steward for God in the distribution of His material blessings. Our money is an instrument expressing our loving response to God's love for us. "We love, because He first loved us" (1 John 4:19). As a consequence, our giving is an expression of our care, concern and eagerness to do God's bidding for the continuation of His work and to meet the needs of the "least of his brethren" (Matthew 25:40). So Christian giving is not done "reluctantly or under compulsion" (2 Corinthians 9:7). That's why it is pleasing to God: "God loves a cheerful giver" (2 Corinthians 9:6). But giving freely as a grateful response to God's many blessings, and as a steward of God's wealth brings much reward to the Christian giver.

Compared to this noble, uplifting and spiritually resourceful concept of giving, the advantages of gambling as a church fundraising method, pale shamefully. Gambling is wrong because it deprives us of the privilege of making our giving a dimension of our spiritual lives. It splits our giving from our commitment to love God, His Church and His people. Gambling is wrong for church and fundraising, not only because of its consequences, but primarily because it appeals to and serves motives which separate it from the essence of what the church is all about: a loving relationship with God and His people.

## 17. THE PATRIARCHATE: AN INTERNATIONAL ORTHODOX CENTER

With the death of the late and beloved Patriarch Athenagoras I, a number of ideas were expressed regarding the location and role of the Ecumenical Patriarchate. Most of all, there has come to the fore a recognition of the fact that the world-wide Orthodox Church needs a center for the coordination of intra-Orthodox activities.

As Orthodoxy has moved into the modern world, it has discovered a need. More than ever before it needs a leader, a coordinating voice, a central focus and a prompter to action. The quick development of ecumenical issues; the lightening communications of our times, and the speed with which problems now develop are commonplaces of our age. They all clearly require the services of a dynamic, concerned central agency to marshall Orthodox Christian response and opinion.

It seems most natural that the Ecumenical Patriarchate be that agency. In 1958 the Greek Orthodox Bishop of the island of Samos proposed that the Ecumenical Patriarchate examine the role of the Orthodox Church in the ecumenical movement so that it could "determine, with the whole weight of the Eastern Orthodox Church, what should be the stance of the Church, and the form of its participation in the World Council of Churches . . . this would cause the fear of disunity among the various autocephalous churches of Orthodoxy to disappear." ("Ekklesia," September 1, 1958, p. 340). Even earlier, in 1936, Professor P. Bratsiotes of the University of Athens proposed that the Ecumenical Patriarchate be developed into a Panorthodox Center with an international character.

Some people object that the Patriarchate is not free to act, since it is in an alien state. The alternatives to this objection do not solve the problem at all, however. It would be conceivable to give the leadership role to another patriarchate—but what is conceivable in theory is inconceivable in practice! Would it be better to submit the center of world Orthodoxy to communist control, Jewish politics or Egyptian Mohammedan influence? Just as difficult an alternative is the suggestion that the Patriarchate function from one of the areas in Greece under its ecclesiastical jurisdiction. It would create serious problems because the church in Greece is subject to the ecclesiastical laws of the State of Greece. Nor could we seriously consider transferring the Patriarchate to another place in the world such as the United States. Such a move would separate the Patriarchate from its historic roots, its faithful and from the nearly 2,000-year tradition which sustains it.

The real answer is the Christian answer! The church is never fully at peace with the world, its rulers or its life, because the church is the Kingdom of the Lord, which by definition is "not of this world." Spiritual leadership will not be formed by geography.

Constantinople enjoys the honor of the "first among equals" in the world-wide Orthodox Church now: by right of canon law, by historical tradition, by spiritual authenticity. All that is needed is for the Ecumenical Patriarchate to vigorously shoulder the responsibilities of world Orthodox leadership. Today, now, and from where it finds itself! The Apostolic Church was also in a less than favorable position in the Roman Empire. Yet, with the power of the Holy Spirit, it led the world into a new age.

Orthodoxy needs world leadership! The mantle of Orthodox leadership belongs to Constantinople, both by tradition and practically. Let the Ecumenical Patriarchate assume the task with vigor, with international perspective and with the apostolic consciousness which has characterized the Patriarchate's whole history! The Orthodox Church throughout the world will follow with gratitude. A good start was the call for a Panorthodox Council to address some contemporary concerns of world Orthodoxy. The movement, however, toward the implementation of the Council has been excruciatingly slow. World Orthodoxy is eager to follow the leadership of the Ecumenical Patriarchate. It need wait for no authority to act decisively and speedily. The Ecumenical Patriarchate already has all the authority and resources it needs.

# Part III

# SEX AND FAMILY ISSUES

## 18. DR. REUBEN'S BOOK ON SEX

The advertisement says "Dr. David Reuben has told forty million readers everything they always wanted to know about sex. Now he tells every woman what to do about men." This second book pretends to continue in the tradition of the first: *Everything You Always Wanted To Know About Sex . . . But Were Afraid To Ask.* If you read the first, you will not want to read the second: the author's views about the meaning of sex in the first make reading the second one not worth the effort.

Dr. Reuben has written a book filled with facts about sex. No honest twentieth century Christian can fault him for that. What Christian wants to return to the hypocritcal mid-victorian views on sex that passed for Christian living during the past centuries? Ignorance is no special virtue, even when it is ignorance of the facts of sex. Certainly, the early Church didn't see it that way.

Christianity, while rich in the development of monastic views on life, also developed very definite views about the goodness and rightness of man's sexual dimension. Marriage was seen as a sacarament and married men were ordained and served at the Holy Altar with the celibates. Those who argued that the body and sex were evil were excommunicated as heretics. The sacrament of Holy Matrimony in the Orthodox Church has many references to the sexual aspects of the new relationship between bride and groom: "for this cause shall a man leave father and mother, and shall cleave unto his wife, and the twain shall be one flesh; and those whom God hath joined together, let no man put asunder." And one father of the church is reputed to have said that "What God was not ashamed to create, you should not be ashamed to speak of!"

## A Pernicious View

So, when Dr. Reuben provides facts about sex, and seeks to answer the legitimate questions of people about the biological and medical aspects of sex, he attempts to do a good thing. But, it must be said with equal candor that he doesn't do that very well. One of the things that mars his book is that Dr. Reuben is not only interested in answering questions, he is also pushing a very pernicious attitude about sex.

Dr. Reuben identifies: (1) sex for the purpose of reproduction; (2) sex for the expression of love; and (3) sex for pleasure (fun-sex). In his view, you have to decide which you want. Dr. Reuben is for number three. His big mistake is in keeping the three aspects apart. Christians have learned that all three must be kept together for sex to have its true fulfillment in human life.

The church has long known and counselled that the proper place for the fulfillment of human sexuality is in the marriage bond. Dr. Reuben's "fun-sex" caters to a view that assigns procreation to marriage, sexual pleasure to un-official or casual liaisons, and has given up as unattainable and impossible sex as an expression of permanent and life-long love. There are many people who think that way. Christians don't.

## The Church's Concern

Orthodox Christianity knows that procreation without the warmth and stability of a loving family is disastrous. The long-time concern of the church for the family has in-tuitively realized what modern psychologists have been re-cently saying: The work of procreation is only begun at the child's birth. Parents are continuously creating life and personality in their children with the kind of family life they provide their children. If parents love each other, and express that love to each other, the sense of being loved and the ability to love is born in their children.

One of many ways that this can happen is when husband and wife express their life-long devotion and love through the union of their bodies in marital sexual relations. God has made us with the sexual drive in us. It seeks fulfillment and completion. When that passion is directed to a person with whom a life-long commitment of love is shared, and when the children brought into life because of that love are nurtured and raised in the warmth of a loving family, then sex achieves a depth which cannot be found elsewhere.

### How About Pleasure?

How about pleasure in sexual relations for husband and wife? Some would argue that there should never be any in a Christian marriage. Unfortunately, for them, that doesn't seem to be the teaching of Christianity. When the husband and wife give pleasure to each other, they are very much in the spirit of what Christian marriage is all about. "Rejoice thou in thy husband" are the words of the marriage ceremony to the new bride. And St. Paul recognizes that sexual desires are properly fulfilled in the marriage relationship when he says, "The husband should give to his wife her conjugal rights, and likewise the wife to her husband . . . Do not refuse one another except perhaps for a season, that you may devote yourselves to prayer; but then come back together again . . . " (1 Cor. 7:3, 5).

The church responds to Dr. Reuben that he, unfortunately, does not have all the answers. Sex is a part of life . . . not separate from it. Sex for reproduction, sex to express love and sex for pleasure are not separate. They are one thing. And the best place they can achieve true fulfillment is in that life-long loving bond made possible by the grace of God: Christian Matrimony!

## 19. PORNOGRAPHY

The Orthodox Church throughout its history has held firmly to the teaching that sex is a God-given human capacity which is properly exercised in marriage. Sexual relations, in the context of marriage, contribute to and express the bond of love of the spouses, meet the bodily needs of the partners and serve creation and nurture of the human race. As a result, for the Church, sex is a blessed and holy part of the life of most persons when practiced in the only setting appropriate to it: marriage. For Orthodox Christians the sacrament of Holy Matrimony clearly places the relation of husband, wife and family in the kingdom of God, blessing and sanctifying all the relationships within the marriage bond, including sexual relations, thus protecting this aspect of life from misuse, abuse, and corrupt distortion. "Let their bed be undefiled," the Church prays in the marriage service. The Church knows and honors, as well, the state of consecrated virginity in which the sexual aspect of life is totally restrained as a sign of devotion and dedication to God. Both the celibate life, and married life, whether they be of clergy or laity are honored and respected by the Church.

### A Sad "New Logic"

Sex, however, in the unredeemed condition in which mankind finds itself, may turn from its proper purposes and readily find improper and inappropriate expressions. One of these is pornography. The secular society finds it difficult to define pornography and to control it. This is because it has strayed from the proper understanding of sex in life. Motivated by hedonism, exaggerated individualism, and a complete misunderstanding of freedom, it has become subject to what Archbishop Iakovos has called the "extravagant thinking and speaking and false reasoning which has become the 'logic of our times.'" (Keynote address, 22nd Clergy Laity Congress, 1974) This "new logic" has led to many changes in the public attitudes of our society regarding sex, and in particular to pornography. The Church's position however has remained clear, direct and unequivocating from the earliest times to the present on this matter.

## The Wisdom of the Old Logic

The early Church responded to the equivalents in those times of "R" and "X" rated films and literature. Clement and Alexandria (3rd century) and St. Gregory of Nyssa (4th century) condemned pictures depicting pornographic scenes. St. John Chrysostom (4th century) strongly condemned the theater of his day which depicted lewd events on the stage. The Council of Trullo (692) in its 100th Canon condemned pictures which incite persons to the enkindling of base pleasure. The Church has a long history of advising against immoral pictures, literature and theatrical presentations and has urged abstention from the use of such sexually stimulating material not only because it arouses passions inappropriately, but also because it distorts the true place of sex in human life.

## Is Pornography a Right?

Much of the public discussion today on the issue of pornography is cast in the framework of constitutional rights in the face of the right of society to protect itself from public immorality. The 1970 Presidential Commission on Obscenity and Pornography which urged the repeal of all legislation on pornography in reference to consenting adults, was generally rejected by the public and has never been implemented. Though Orthodox Christianity supports the value of freedom and individual rights, it also recognizes that there are limits to those rights. Orthodoxy, in particular, is sensitive to the need to maintain a climate in society as a whole which will foster those values which encourage family, home, and marriage. As a Church, we are concerned about the increasing display and distribution of materials which degrade, trivialize and cheapen sex,taking from it, its God-given sanctity and removing it from its God-given context and framework: marriage and family. We are rapidly becoming a "pornographic society" in which the individual is immersed in an atmosphere which corrupts and distorts. As a Church, we are alarmed at this tendency which we see as threatening the spiritual and emotional well-being of our children. Further, the genuine meaning of sex in relation to the whole pattern of love in marriage is undermined. It is clear that this emphasis on hedonistic indulgence will further weaken the fabric of our nation and society, threatening its order and survival.

## A Public Stance

Orthodox Christians must become fully aware that pornography is not in any way compatible with our belief that each of us is called to grow in the image and likeness of God toward theosis. As citizens we must oppose the spread of pornography in films, on television, in books, periodicals and other print media. Since this is such a widespread phenomenon, Orthodox Christians will want to work together with other concerned persons in ecumenical efforts to limit this social evil. Where such cooperation exists already the Orthodox Church through its pastors and laity will want to "expand its participation in the various movements and commissions to eliminate pornography." (Clergy-Laity Congress, 1970). This means that as a Church we support civil laws which reduce the exposure of society in general to pornographic materials. We understand the problem of the conflict between the demands of public morality and the rights of adults in our pluralistic society. We believe, however, that the laws of our nation ought to have a bias toward supporting the stability of the family and wholesome attitudes toward sex in our society.

## A Wholesome Attitude

Finally, as a Church, we must develop in our children a
wholesome Christian attitude to the place of sex in their
lives as future husbands, wives, and parents. This is not
only the appropriate way for them to live their our Christian lives, but it will contribute to a wholesome environment for the future of the Church and society in general. As
St. John Chrysostom noted, speaking on the proper upbringing of children, "the root being made good, good
branches will shoot forth, and still become better, and for
all these you will receive a reward." Happy lives, in which
sex is seen as a divine blessing uniting husband and wife in
complete union, as well as an orderly, undistorted and
happy society will be the reward.


## 20. THE V.D. EPIDEMIC: A SURE CURE

According to some statistics, venereal disease is the second most widespread illness in the United States today:
only the common cold has more victims. Public health
agencies, private physicians, teen self-help groups and
others, have mobilized to provide information and assistance to the afflicted.

### Current Tactics

Many kinds of tactics are used to deal with the problem. Some emphasize the terrible results of the various
forms of VD, especially if left untreated. Others push the
idea that VD is not too serious and relatively easy to cure,
if treated early. The first approach seeks to frighten the
prospective victim, while the second seeks to motivate him
or her to seek out medical assistance. Further, all kinds of
advice is proffered to the young on how to avoid Syphilis
and Gonorrhea.

A recent article in a national women's magazine called

the incidence of VD in the U.S. a "pandemic" and offered
as the cure a combination of better sex education courses,
drop-in centers, VD telephone hot lines, ready availability
to medical treatment (wherever possible, without parental
knowledge) and other such devices.

## Avoiding the Issue

That article was not unique. A quick survey of the popular articles in national magazines, as well as the kinds of
information provided in many sex-education courses and
hot-line services will convince you that the one sure cure
for venereal disease is nearly always ignored, or presented
as the "least desirable alternative." The VD pandemic
would rapidly diminish in numbers of infected people and
in intensity, if the avoidance of premarital sexual relations
were accepted as the "most desirable" approach to the
problem. But, in fact, our society at large is hotly encouraging all kinds of sexual expression as it seeks to break
down the traditional moral structure.

In an almost schizophrenic exercise, America is in-
structing youth in the techniques of premarital sexual
practices, while at the same time it decries the widespread
incidence of Syphilis and Gonorrhea. In fact, the contemporary evaluation of the situation is really saying that virginity and premarital continence is too high a price to pay
in order to overcome the pandemic of VD.

## Facing the Issue

Not so with the Christian Church. It must first be
pointed out categorically and clearly that the church, especially in the East, has always held that sex and marriage
belong together as a holy, a blessed thing. Though virginity
and continence for life have always been praised, marriage
has consistently been defended and supported. The Orthodox Church has never held the so-called "victorian" view
that sex was dirty or impure in itself.

What the church has said from the beginning is that human sexual relations are part of a larger whole. Sex is important, but it is not the most important part of being human. Sex has a significant place in the total pattern of life, but it is not at the center of life. The church teaches that God stands at the center of life. Being human means being related to Him and living a "new life" in which love for God, our fellow human beings and ourselves are integrated in a style of life appropriate to a follower of Christ.

Sex has its appropriate and fitting place in the whole scheme of human life. And that place is marriage. The whole pattern of love, personal commitment, "growth into wholeness," maturity, mutual support, birth of children, the nurture and education of children, care for ever-increasing pre-adult life, and finally, emotional and physical support for aged parents, supports the view that the holiness of sex should not be blasphemed outside of marriage.

### A Sure Cure

There is a sure cure to the VD epidemic: premarital continence by both men and women. Remaining pure sexually is the best antiseptic and the most effective antibiotic. It is never too late to make the decision. A Mary Magdalene, a Saint Augustine, and a Holy Mary of Egypt are only three examples from a host of saints who regained their purity after many failures. For those who have not fallen, there is an important decision to be made: the love of God and *His* way, or the distorted popular misconceptions of the present day.

Saint Paul gives every young person today the guidelines that are needed:

*"Let us cast off the works of darkness and put on the armor of light; let us conduct ourselves becomingly as in the day, not in reveling and drunkenness, not in fornication and licentiousness . . . " (Romans 13:12-13).*

> *"Now the works of the flesh are plain: adultery, fornication, licentiousnesss, sorcery, enmity, strife, jealousy, anger, selfishness, dissention . . . those who do such things shall not inherit the kingdom of God" (Galatians 5:19-20).*
>
> *"Let no one despise your youth, but set the believers an example in speech and conduct, in love, in faith, in purity" (1 Timothy 4:12).*

## 21. THE ORTHODOXY OF CONTRACEPTION

A while ago, the "Orthodox Observer" the newspaper of the Greek Orthodox Archdiocese carried a long article on the issue of contraception from an Orthodox point of view. A number of letters from readers indicated a significant divergence of opinion as to the Orthodoxy of the opinions expressed in the article. The author of that article the V. Rev. Chrysostom Zafiris, does not need to be defended by this writer. Rather, it is important to view the responses to this article so as to understand the nature of the discussion and to arrive at a conclusion on the Orthodox view regarding contraception, or birth control.

### Two Approaches, Two Methods, Two Answers

Within modern Orthodox Christianity, varying views on the subject exist. They can, however, be classified in two basic approaches, with methods and conclusions appropriate to each. Father Zafiris' article is characteristic of one approach. A book written in Greek a number of years ago by Fr. Seraphim Papacostas, entitled *To Zetema tis Tecknogonias* (The Issue Concerning Child-Bearing), represents the other approach.

What should be noted at the beginning is that this lack of clarity has its roots in some of the traditions of the church itself. Basically, it is to be found in a varying understanding of sex in the life of the Christian. Searching the tradition, we receive the impression that sex is, on the one hand, a God-created distinction of persons through which men and women share in the creative work of God, a God-given desire and attraction which serves to unite a husband and wife into a psychosomatic unity. The Apostle Paul sees the sexual relations of husband and wife as required to ward off temptation. The church has designated the blessing of the marital relationship as a sacrament. Those who have condemned sex and marriage as evil and debasing have, in turn, been condemned by the church in numerous church canons. On the one hand, then, as the service of Holy Matrimony says, "marriage is honorable and the bed undefiled."

However, at the same time the powerful influence of monasticism has tended not only to lower the estimation of the married life, but also to equate sex in general to a condition not quite fitting and appropriate for Christians, if not, in fact, sinful. At its extreme, this view held that marriage itself was nothing but "legalized fornication."

Both these views have been held and promulgated through the years within the church, even though they are mutually inconsistent. This inconsistency has been reflected in approaches to the question of contraception.

### "Natural Law" View

Some of the tradition has emphasized the biological dimensions of sex in marriage, tending to see its place in the scheme of things as a basically evil passion which, however, is needed to propagate the race. Thus, sex is tied closely to a view of natural law which sees a biological purpose as the crucial factor.

The result of this approach is two-fold: sexual relations are seen as legitimate only when the intended purpose is to conceive and bear children; sexual relations entered into for pleasure, for the purpose of expressing love or deepening the marital relationship, are simply not considered relevant or seen as positively violating the natural and legitimate purpose of sexual relations. Thus, any method which circumvents the only admitted purpose for sexual relations in marriage, such as contraception, is morally wrong. This is the approach taken by the book *To Zetema tis Teknogonias* and some of the letter-writers who made frequent appeals to "the natural law."

## Sacramental View

The approach of Fr. Zafiris' article and that supported in Fr. John Meyendorff's book, *Marriage: An Orthodox Perspective,* as well as Fr. Demetrios Constantelos' book *Marriage, Sexuality and Celebacy: A Greek Orthodox Perspective* places the emphasis for the meaning of sex in general and contraception in particular on the whole experience of marriage as a holy,interpersonal relationship within the total framework of the Christian life. This approach sees marriage and the sex within it as having many purposes, none of which is seen as the crucial and exclusive purpose. When marriage and the sexual relations within it are approached from this sacramental perspective, then sexual relations between husband and wife are procreative in purpose, but also unitive.

In this perspective the sexual relations of husband and wife have an intrinsic value: they unite husband and wife in flesh and soul in a bond of mutual love and commitment. The procreative purpose remains, however. But when children have been born, and the task is now the nurture of those children in a family environment of mutual love and in an atmosphere dominated by the relationship of the husband and wife, that sexual relationship is also significant for the whole tenor and well-being of the family life. Within this perspective contraception is not condemned, but rather it is seen as a means for the furthering of the goals and purposes of marriage as understood by the church. Normally, it would be wrong to use contraceptives to avoid the birth of *any* children. However, once children have been born, the use of contraceptives by the parents does not seem to violate any fundamental Christian understanding of marriage.

### Which Is More Correct?

As we have indicated, there is evidence in the history of the church to provide support for both approaches. That is why there is still discussion and controversy. Even our archdiocese has responded differently at different times. In older issues of the archdiocese *Yearbook* a strong negative attitude was expressed. In more recent issues, a position was taken indicating that this was a private matter, involving the couple alone, which was to be discussed with the Father Confessor.

The real issue is which of the two views best represents the fulness of the Orthodox Christian Faith. The first, negative response, draws primarily on an exclusively biological, physical and legalistic perspective. The second, affirmative response, emphasizes the close relationship of body and soul, places the issue in the total context of marriage and family, and most importantly, takes a sacramental approach. To state the differences of emphasis is to respond to the question "Which Is More Correct?" The second fits a well-rounded Orthodox Christian view of the truth.

It should be clearly stated that for the church, sexual relations outside of marriage are sinful and the use of contraceptives merely compounds the impropriety of that kind of behavior. Nor should anything said above imply that there is an obligation on the part of couples to use contraceptives if they do not wish to. What we are saying is that if a married couple has children, or is spacing the birth of their children, and wishes to continue sexual relations in the subsequent years as an expression of their continuing love for each other, and for the deepening of their personal and marital unity, the Orthodoxy of contraception is affirmed.

## 22. THE ORTHODOX CHRISTIAN VIEW ON ABORTION

One of the most threatening social and moral problems facing our nation today is the ever-increasing prevalence and acceptance of abortion. Three out of every ten pregnancies in America end with the deliberate expulsion and death of the human fetus. That adds up to more than one million abortions each year. Furthermore, many of our Christian brethren of other Churches are heard declaring abortion to be an individual right under Christian freedom.

In the light of these awesome realities, it is necessary to express the position of our Eastern Orthodox Church in regard to the complex problem of abortion as found embodied in her great historical, theological, and moral tradition. There is need to settle the hearts and minds of our Orthodox faithful who are being forced to deal with this issue with increasing frequency.

### Early Condemnation

Since the earliest days of her existence, the Christian Church has consistently declared willful abortion of a human fetus to be equivalent to murder. St. Basil in the fourth century declared that, "Those who give potions for the destruction of the child conceived in the womb are murderers; as are they who take the poisons which kill the child (8th canon of St. Basil)."

Thus, if we are to give trustworthy response to the intricate questions provoked by the abortion controversy arising in our own era, we must give heed to the theological and ethical concerns which guided the early Church in formulating her pronouncements. We must remember as well that her counsel arose out of a spirit of love and a consequent pastoral concern for the moral and spiritual well-being of the Christian flock.

## Our Faith Provides the Reasons

As Orthodox Christians, we profess that all life comes from God and that human life represents the most precious gift that our Creator has bestowed upon us. That God Himself places ultimate value on the sanctity of human life is evident by the fact that out of His great love for us, "He gave His only-begotten Son, that whoever believes in Him should not perish but have eternal life" (John 3:16).

Human life is not an unconditional gift from God, but carries with it certain responsibilities. That God considers the taking of an innocent life to be a particularly heinous crime is evident, not only from the Sixth Commandment, but also from the story of Cain and Abel recounted in Genesis 4:1-6. Further, the Incarnation of the Logos has, for all eternity, sanctified all human life, in both its physical and spiritual aspects.

In his creation, man is given the imprint of God's own image and likeness; Adam's fall shattered the image and destroyed the likeness but through the Second Adam's Life, Death and Resurrection the image is mended and the likeness restored. This means, not only that human existence and personhood mirrors the Divine, but also that we all have the potential of growing more and more like God until we reach union with Him. This transformation involves the whole human person, body and soul, as witnessed by the transfigured and uncorruptible flesh of the Resurrected Christ.

Finally, since God is perfect beyond our human comprehension, the process of growing more like God, of "developing our personhood", is a never ending one for every human being. It begins at conception and continues to the very moment of our physical death. Thus, no human being is a "person" or entirely "human" in the fullest sense, since none of us are exactly like God. Yet all human beings share the same potential developing into "persons" whether they be in the womb, at the prime of life, or on their deathbed. The potential for "personhood" of the human fetus is evident not only from the Orthodox concept of psychosomatic unity, but from Scripture. As Orthodox, we believe that the Divine Logos came to occupy the human body of Jesus from the moment of conception (Luke 1:26-38); and Mary's cousin Elizabeth, the mother of St. John the Baptist, testifies that "the babe in my womb leaped for joy" (Luke 1:44) when she heard the sound of the Virgin Mary's voice.

### Is Abortion a Woman's Right?

One of the most common arguments used by supporters of abortion on demand is that a woman's right to privacy extends to control over what happens within her own body, including the contents of her uterus. This argument was accepted by the Supreme Court (as far as the first three months of pregnancy are concerned) in its 1973 decision on abortion. Some advocates of this position go so far as to refer to the nascent life as a cancerous growth, or "piece of extraneous tissue", that has invaded the mother's womb. Orthodoxy rejects such notions due to the great value attached to life by God, and the fact that life is a gift which no persons has the right to take. If we do not have the right to take our own lives, how much more so must it be that we have no right to take the innocent life of the embryo or fetus in the womb? If our bodies are "temples of the Holy Spirit" as we profess, then to kill an innocent human being is a crime, not only against that person, but also against the Holy Spirit. That the developing persons inside the mother's womb has a life separate from its mother is evident from the fact that its chromosomal makeup is different from the mother's since it is a combination drawn from both mother and father. Further, it is genetically unique; its particular combination of traits and characteristics shall never be repeated.

## Is the Fetus a Person?

A second argument commonly made by those who favor abortion "rights" is that, particularly if the removal of the nascent life occurs during the first few weeks of pregnancy, no human person, or person who is "fully human" has been destroyed. They also claim that unwanted children will not have the opportunity of developing into "responsible personhood," or will jeopardize the "personhood" of parents and siblings, due to the added burden they impose. In opposition, we profess that no human being is ever fully a "person", but that all persons have the potential to become "fully human", to achieve union with God. Therefore, we cannot declare on the basis of "personhood" that the fetus in the womb has no value, or lesser value in the eyes of both God and man than a person born.

## Are Exceptions Possible?

When the life of the mother is in jeopardy due to her pregnancy, then an exception to the prohibition on abortion may be allowed. Such situations are always tragic, particularly for the mother—who faces the terrible choice between her own life and that of the child growing within her. But here, the particular circumstances of the situation (e.g., terminally ill mother, or existence of several other children who would be orphaned) must be taken into consideration, in a spirit of Christian love and sacrifice. It is certainly senseless for both lives to be lost. Any decision of this sort should be made by the woman in consultation with her medical and spiritual advisors, as well as the father of the child.

In cases of rape or incest, due to the unnatural and often violent character of these crimes, as well as the danger of disease, it is urged that medical procedures take place as soon as possible to flush out the sperm before fertilization or implantation can occur. Young women should be instructed that such action take place immediately (no later than 3 days after impregnation). But once implantation occurs, the pregnant woman should carry the child to term, and the alternative of adoption should be approached in a spirit of Christian love.

In cases where the possibilities are high, or it is definitely known that the child will be born severely deformed or retarded, no exception can be made. Even such human beings are created in the image of and likeness of God. At the same time, however, no couple should be forced to bear the financial, emotional, or social burden that falls on those parents of such "exceptional children". The Orthodox Church should lend its support to any legislation which would provide funds and adequate facilities for the care of these persons in a nurturing environment.

No other exceptions are acceptable reasons for permitting abortions. The Church emphasizes, however, that all women involved in problem pregnancies deserve to be treated with compassion, Christian love, and pastoral understanding. The possibility of giving the child up to an adoption agency should be suggested, and the stigma attached to such a sacrifice, usually made for the welfare of the child and not the convenience of the mother, should be actively opposed. Support should be provided for the unwed mother, as well as a place of residence, if none exists. We cannot insist on the necessity to avoid abortion, if we do not at the same time provide an environment of Christian nurture and safety to both mother and child. It was the fourth century father of the church, St. Basil, who noted that regarding abortion "there is involved the question of providing justice for the infant to be born" (2nd Canon). Those women who in human weakness opt for abortion, should be welcomed back into the Christian fold in a spirit of love and forgiveness if they sincerely repent of their sin with the understanding that we are all subject to sin.

## Political Action

For the Orthodox, the Ecumenical Council is the highest authority. The sixth Ecumenical Council, held in the year 691, decreed in its ninety-first canon the following: "As for women who furnish drugs for the purpose of procuring abortion and those who take fetus-killing poisons, they are made subject to the penalty prescribed for murderers." Several other canons and pronouncements of church fathers, very similar to the above canon, have embedded in Orthodox Christian teaching the conviction that abortion is an act, regardless of the means employed, of the unjust killing of a human being, that is, of murder. For the Orthodox Christian Church, it is incomprehensible how a well-ordered state can permit, tolerate or encourage any form of murder. Rather, it is the duty and responsibility of the state to protect the innocent and the weak.

As members of the Orthodox Church, therefore we should consider it our duty to support proper political efforts aimed at prohibiting abortion, except in extreme circumstances. We should also support any legislation aimed at assisting unwed or unsupported pregnant women, or to disseminate information, with a Christian orientation, with the purpose of preventing unwanted pregnancies from occurring in the first place. Orthodoxy affirms that the only proper place for conjugal love is within the bounds of Holy Matrimony, but express our sympathy and understanding to those who bear the unfortunate consequences of not adhering to this moral precept. It is therefore obvious that the Orthodox Christian Church, whose position on this issue has stood the test of two thousand years of its history, stands opposed today to all efforts to continue to make abortion the permitted practice of this nation.

## 23. EMBRYO FERTILIZATION OUTSIDE THE WOMB

The startling birth of Louise Brown, the first known "test-tube" baby in England gave added urgency to an already existing need for an Orthodox Christian comment of artificial insemination. Furthermore, the case of Louise Brown was unique in that the child was conceived outside and then implanted in the mother's womb. There is need to provide guidelines based on Orthodox belief, for our Orthodox Christians so as to determine if artificial insemination and/or *in vitro fertilization* is permissible under any circumstances, and to provide a framework for dealing with future problems arising from fast-moving scientific development. These lines seek to provide this direction until some more official response is formulated by the Church.

### Basic Positions

The Orthodox Church affirms the duty of the procreation of the human race, as our Creator commanded that man "Be fruitful and multiple and fill the earth" (Gen. 1:28). She is also aware of the added responsibility given to man in the second charge of managing his own reproductive behavior, to "subdue" the earth and "have dominion over every living thing" (Gen. 1:28-29). Herein can be found the answers to such modern issues as "maintaining the balance of nature" and "guarding against overpopulation."

The Church also stresses the sacramental character of Christian marriage; in the Sacrament of Matrimony, natural marriage enters the realm of God's eternal Kingdom. Within its bounds, husband and wife are called to perfect their love for one another into a life-long communion and to grow in oneness towards Christ. And out of this mutual love of husband and wife for one another, all other purposes of marriage flow. Husband and wife pledge their mutual support to one another not only in the joy of life but also in trials and tribulations. They exclusively provide for one another's sexual fulfillment in an all-embracing love.

## The Meaning of Children

As the Christian couple progresses in love, they find themselves growing closer, both to each other and to God. The eventual birth of their children is an eloquent and significant expression and seal of their loving union. For their offspring represent not only the physical (genetic) union of husband and wife, but also in their spiritual union, the presence of God, the one true source of the love in their marriage. Here they share with God in the creation of new human beings: with the Son who creates according to the will of God the Father, and with the Holy Spirit who imparts the vivifying grace of God to the child conceived. The new family represents a little "ekklesia" or "church", a magnificent manifestation of Christ's love.

## Artificial Insemination

This sacramental unity of marriage and the family is maintained as long as no foreign party sunders the unique bond between husband and wife. It excludes all intrusions such as if a third party joins one of the spouses in sexual relations, but also when the seal of marriage is broken by an outside party contributing genetic material (whether semen or ovum) towards the creation of a child who ought to belong genetically to not one but both marriage partners.

For the same reason, in principle, the Church holds it morally wrong for the ovum (egg) of another woman to be impregnated by the sperm of the husband artificially and implanted in the wife's womb. The obligation to preserve the bond of marital fidelity thus prohibits Orthodox Christians from the practice of artificial imsemination by a donor in which the wife of a sterile husband is impregnated through a medical procedure with the sperm of an anonymous male donor. However, the Orthodox Church, recognizing as it does the importance of the procreative function, ought not to offer direct opposition to the procedure of artificial insemination where the procedure respects the bounds of marital fidelity. This means the egg must come from the wife's own ovaries, and that the sperm must be the husband's own; for a donor, whether male or female, would constitute the intrusion of a third party into the marriage tantamount to adultery.

What permits this rather unusual practice is that it is a way in which medical knowledge is properly used to help the Christian marriage realize one of its major purposes: procreation. There does not seem to be any major moral problem with the relatively simple process by which artificial insemination takes place. The methods by which the semen is obtained from the husband for this purpose are clinical and medical in nature, whose motive and intent distinguish them fully from similar acts done with totally different motives, intents and purposes (masturbation).

## Test Tube Babies

However, *in vitro fertilization* (test tube babies) according to which the ovum and the sperm are united outside the wife's body present serious problems to the Orthodox conscience. In this procedure the cells which produce the ova (oocytes) are removed from the wife's body, fertilized by the sperm of husband or donor, kept in a laboratory culture solution until they reach a certain stage of development (blastocyte stage) and subsequently transferred and implanted in the mother's womb. Serious objection is raised here to the fact that many more eggs are fertilized than can be use; those not used are discarded. This is easily seen to be the killing of potential life: abortion. Though there are a few cases of well-born test-tube babies, we do not know the effects of this procedure on all children who would be born from these methods. We do know that many deformities can and have taken place in test-tube experiments. Finally, objections must be raised in terms of the mentality created by such a practice. As a step which de-humanizes life and which separates so dramatically the personal relations of a married couple from child-bearing it is very suspect. For the above mentioned reasons, it would seem that the Orthodox Church should not encourage its members to become involved in *invitro fertilization* procedures, nor does it seem that it would be wise for society in general to encourage this practice.

### No Children Possible?

In the case of men and women who have been rendered sterile and who cannot benefit from a fertilization procedure excluding all but genetic material from husband and wife, the Church expresses sympathy but upholds the sanctity of the marriage bond against outside intrusion. A couple faced with such a problem should be directed toward adoption as an alternative, especially in light of our contemporary overpopulation problems. The Church would for the same reason also have to reject any future use of a "host mother" in whom a fertilized egg could be implanted until the fetus developed to term, at which time the child would be turned over to its genetic parents. Such a procedure is foreseen to be used when a woman cannot carry a child to term due to uterine problems or defects, or if she simply wishes to avoid the inconveniences of pregnancy and child-bearing. This procedure seems especially contrary to Orthodox Christian ethic in view of the special, natural, spiritual, and emotional relationship which exists between mother and baby during pregnancy.

### Artificial Wombs

If an artificial womb were to be developed making it possible to support human life entirely outside a human mother's womb, while no third party is technically present

here, it would seem that the Church would also oppose this
procedure as contrary to nature and as a sorry attempt by
creatures to mimic a function unique to their Creator. Such
an action would also constitute a denial of the fullness of
our physical existence which is sanctified by our Lord's Incarnation and consecrated to God's service in all its aspects
including the sexual and reproductive functions. In opposing a substitute womb, whether human or mechanical, the
Church seeks to protect the mental and spiritual welfare of
the unborn child: the child of a "host mother" or artificial
womb is a candidate for severe identity problems: Who is
his mother—his "genetic" or "host" mother? And is a child
of an artificial womb human, or machine? Indeed, the
sanctity of the mother's womb must be maintained if we
are to fully maintain our humanity.

## 24. HOMOSEXUALITY

The Orthodox Church has long had a clear and firmly
articulated position regarding homosexual acts. It has not
had as clear a position on homosexuality as a condition
since the distinction between homosexual acts and the
homosexual condition is the result of recent developments
in scientific knowledge. An objective definition and understanding of homosexuality is difficult to come by because
of the widespread controversy on the issue in the scientific,
religious, ethical and public sphere. One that comes close
to being neutral and balanced, reflecting modern knowl-
edgeable opinion is the following:

> *Homosexuality is . . . a predominant, persistent, and
> exclusive psychosexual attraction toward members of
> the same sex. A homosexual person is one who feels
> sexual desire for and a sexual responsiveness to per-
> sons of the same sex and who seeks or would like to
> seek actual sexual fulfillment of this desire by sexual*

*acts with a person of the same sex. (Encyclopedia of Bioethics Vol. 2, p. 671).*

This definition points to a clear distinction between homosexual acts and a conditon in a person attracting them to these acts.

## Homosexual Acts

Regarding homosexual acts, the traditional and exclusive teaching of the Church is condemnatory, seeing such acts as morally wrong. In the face of homosexual acts as well as all other expressions of wrongful sexual expression (fornication, adultery, prostitution, incest, bestiality, masturbation) the Church teaches that the only proper place for the exercise of the sexual function is in marriage. The evidence from the sources of the faith, without exception, considers homosexual acts as morally wrong. In the Old Testament, we read "If there is a man who lies with a male as those be with a woman, both of them have committed a detestable act. (Leviticus 20:13. Also, 18:22). Grave punishment was visited on the city of Sodom by God for this sin (Genesis 19:1-29) and as a result Sodomy is another name by which homosexual behavior is described. In speaking of this sinful act, the New Testament uses it to illustrate the "depraved passions" of fallen humanity: "their women exchanged the natural function for that which is unnatural, and in the same way the men abandoned the natural function of women and burned in their desire towards one another, men with men, commiting indecent acts . . . " (Romans 1:24-28). Elsewhere, this evil is related with several others and severe punishment is promised: "Do you not know that the unrighteous will not inherit the kingdom of God? Do not be deceived; neither the immoral, nor idolaters, nor adulterers, nor homosexuals (arsenokoitai — literally, "men go to bed with men for sexual acts"), nor thieves, nor the greedy, nor drunkards, nor revilers, nor robbers will inherit the kingdom of God" (1 Corinthians

6:9-10. Also, 1 Timothy 1:8-10).

The patristic tradition is no less unanimous and clear-cut in its judgment. From the 2nd century *Didache of the Twelve Apostles,* through the writings of the Fathers of the Golden Age of the Church such as St. Basil, St. John Chrysostom, St. Augustine, St. Gregory of Nyssa (4th and 5th centuries), through the sixth century Code of Justinian, the *Canons* of St. John the Faster (early 7th century) to the decisions of the 21st (1972), and 23rd (1976) Clergy-Laity statement on Homosexuality by the Standing Conference of Canonical Orthodox Bishops in the Americas, released in March of 1978, the teaching is consistant and unvarying: homosexual acts are immoral and wrong.

## The Homosexual Condition

The distinction made between homosexual condition and homosexual acts, however, addresses the pastoral concerns of the Church regarding persons who are subject to "exclusive psychosexual attraction towards members of the same sex." In the language of the Church, this is a "passion". It is a wrongful orientation of our desires. Passions are of many kinds, directed toward many objects, such as self (pride), money (greed), food (gluttony), extra-marital sex partners (lust), others' property (theft), etc. When such passions exist, no matter how strongly felt, the Church counsels *agona*, that is, spiritual and moral struggle against them. In our commonly shared struggle against sin in whatever form, the Orthodox Church sees all persons working to fight temptation and overcome the passions. Toward this end the Church offers a panoply of spiritual weapons to overcome temptations and to struggle victoriously against the passions. These spiritual weapons including prayer, worship, fasting, the Sacrament of Holy Confession, reading of Scripture and of patristic and spiritual writings, Christian fellowship, as well as pastoral and psychiatric counseling which should be used by all including those who suffer from homosexual tendencies. The Church must increase its pastoral concern for the homosexual who seeks to eliminate homosexual acts from his or her life and to do this it must minister as a whole, through its pastors and people, to those who enter into this struggle sincerely and honestly. The Church should do this with the same compassion, love and sensitivity as it does with all others who struggle to overcome and to grow in Christ.

## Gay Rights

In the light of the current debate regarding "Gay Rights" the Orthodox Church will agree and support guarantees to the basic rights due all persons of life, and dignity, liberty, basic needs and equal access to them. However, for the protection and care of others, the Orthodox Church cannot join in advocacy efforts which will legalize homosexual acts, or encourage public display of homosexually related behavior. In its own Canon law, it prohibits homosexuals from becoming priests. (Canon 19, John the Faster; Canon 4, Cyril of Alexandria). By extension, the Orthodox Church does not favor the employment of those who have homosexual tendencies in positions such as teachers and youth counsellors, where there is constant close contact with children. The overt practice of homosexuality, its public acceptance as an "alternative life-style", the effort to make prideful that which is shameful are condemned by the Orthodox Church and seen as a severe attack on the family. The general position of the Orthodox Church is, therefore, summed up in the March 7, 1978 statement on Homosexuality issued by the Standing Conference of Canonical Orthodox Bishops in the Americas: "The Christian family is currently subject to serious negative pressures from secular elements in our society. Such are the extensive campaigns of self-proclaimed homosexuals, both individually and collectively, to obtain recognition of their life-styles as being of equal worth with marriage and the home. Without wishing to penalize anyone who deserves sympathy and pastoral assistance from the Christian community because of physical or emotional personality states over which they have no control, the Standing Conference of Canonical Orthodox Bishops in the Americas reiterates the clear directives of scriptures and tradition which condemn voluntary homosexual acts as sinful and forbidden and detrimental to the existence of the Christian home. Persons who embrace homosexual lifestyles are not qualified to teach children or act as spiritual leaders."

## 25. TRANSEXUALS

In 1978 the Greek Orthodox Archdiocese was petitioned for a marriage license by a couple, one of whom had had a sex change operation. This raised for the Church serious questions of theological, ethical, canonical and sacramental nature. What are transexuals, how does the Church look upon this condition and should the sacramental marriage of transexuals be permitted in the Orthodox Church?

### What Is a Transexual?

In asking the question "What are transexuals?" modern approaches to sexuality must first be understood. "Biological sex" is the phrase which indicates the anatomical structures which characterize males and females. "Gender Identity" is the internalized role of either male or female with which our inner being identifies. The vast majority of persons identify their gender (maleness or femaleness) with their biological sex. Another phrase, "sexual orientation" refers to persons whose biological and gender sexual identity is the same (for example, a biological male who identifies himself as a male) but who "feels sexual desire for and a sexual responsiveness to persons of the same sex." Such persons are homosexuals.

There is, however, in a small number of persons another, distinct, condition in which biological sex and gender identity differ. In such situations, for example, a biological male has strong gender confusion and in varying measure has a female psychological identity. This is known as "transvestism." Transvestites range in intensity from occasional and passing expressions, such as privately wearing feminine clothing to stronger public expressions of this mixed sexual identity condition. It appears more frequently among biological males, than among biological females. In a very small number of people there is such a confusion of biological sex and gender identity, and the conflict is so persistent and great, that they feel the tremendous need to physically alter their biological sex in order that it conform with their psychological gender identity. Recently, surgical operations have been developed to respond to this desire.

### Sex Change Operations

Persons who have this confused condition in such strong intensity are often referred to as transexuals. Nearly all those who seek sex-change operations are transexuals though others may also seek them for different psychological reasons. The operation itself began to be developed in pre-WWII Germany and was popularized in December of 1952 with an operation in Denmark on Christine Jorgensen. In the USA the leader in the development of the operation, sometimes called "sex-reassignment surgery" or "transmogrification" was Johns Hopkins University Medical School. The operation consists, for males, of a procedure in which the male sexual organs are removed and replaced with surgical approximations of female organs and it is followed by hormonal treatments. The reverse procedure (female to male) is much more difficult and more rarely done.

Considered widely to be still an experimental procedure, Johns Hopkins University, followed by a number of
other hospitals in the United States, has stopped the procedure. Responsible studies have concluded that sex-reassignment surgery, though responsive to a desire of transexuals, in fact, has had little or no effect on the sex identity of
the patients, resolving few if any of the conflicts, and in
some cases causing more problems because of the irrevers-
ability of the operation.

## The Church's View

How should the Church look upon transexualism? It is
evident that the confusion of biological sex and sexual
gender identity is perceived as something abnormal. There
is nothing in the literature of the faith which specifically
addresses this psychological condition. However, we do
have in the tradition criticism and moral disapproval of
practices associated with transvestism as expressed in the
wearing of clothing appropriate to the opposite sex. Thus
the Old Testament says, "A woman shall not wear anything that pertains to a man, nor shall a man put on a
woman's garment; for whoever does these is an abomina-
tion unto the Lord." (Deuteronomy 22:5) In the Canons of
the Church we read "If for the sake of supposedly ascetic
practice any woman change apparel and instead of the
usual and customary women's apparel she dons men's apparel, let her be anathema" (Council of Gangra, Canon 13
A.A. 340). Further, the Church has condemned castration
which is the ancient practice by which young boys were
surgically deprived of their testes and thus rendered both
sterile and effeminate. This was seen by some as a form of
suicide and condemned by the Canons (Holy Apostles, Canon 22 and Canon 24). It was repeated by the 1st Ecumenical Council 325. The 5th-6th Council held in Constantinople in 861, made an exception however for such operations
in the case of illness, "for we consider this to be a treatment

of a disease, but not a malicious design against the ceature or an insult to creation" (Canon 8). In each case the rationale does not address the psychological problem of transexualism but other issues such as physical sexual integrity, respect for creation, the protection of physical life and health. Perhaps, on the basis of the last quoted canon, giving exception for health reasons, a sex reassignment operation might be considered as a compassionate form of therapy for such persons and not seen as "a design against the creature or an insult to creation." However, given the present state of scientific knowledge and the general failure of such operations to resolve the psychological condition, such encouragement would appear to be misdirected. For the Church, then, the transexual condition is an illness, a sad and sorrowful psychological condition. The Church counsels such persons to work with the appropriate therapeutic agencies to avail themselves of the spiritual resources of the Church so as to deal with their affliction; the Church urges these persons to put their trust daily in God for strength to address their problem, and never to despair and lose hope.

## Is a Transexual Marriage Right?

Should someone have had this operation, can the Church marry them in the Sacrament of Holy Matrimony? The Church acknowledges numerous purposes for marriage: procreation of children, mutual help and support, satisfaction of sexual needs, and growth in love. Further, the Church only knows and permits as natural, marriage between a man and a woman. It would seem that all the conditions of a genuine marriage cannot in such cases be fulfilled by persons who have had sex-reorientation operations. In addition, the confusion of sex and gender has not, in fact, been obliterated by such operations as scientific evidence seems to indicate (for example, transmogrified males may continue to shave as usual after the operation;

and biological women who have had the operation cannot have an erection). Whatever sexual satisfaction exists in such relationships, is, in the words of one researcher "95% psychological." In much less drastic circumstances the Church considers marriage inappropriate (Canon 87 of St. Basil on impediments to marriage). The Orthodox Church could not remain consistent with its general marriage practice and bless such relationships in the Sacrament of marriage. Those who have had such operations for their psychological well-being should develop companionship in other kinds of normal and wholesome patterns of relationship, seeking to live out their lives, as all Orthodox pray they may, "in peace" so that "the end of our lives may be Christian, without undue suffering, without shame, peaceful; and for a good account of ourselves before the awesome tribunal of Christ."

## 26. UNDER ATTACK: THE FAMILY

It seems that the family, its values and its stability are under continuing attack by our society. When the family is understood to be the "building block" of society, the developments in our laws and the legal interpretations of existing laws during the past several years seem to be directed at its dissolution.

Just look at what is happening! The family, as the monogamous relationship of one man and one woman for the procreation of children, mutual love and support, and personal union, has everything stacked against it in this society! Even more is the family seen to be under attack when, from our Orthodox Christian viewpoint, the family is understood as a network of sacramental relationships: marriage, baptism, confirmation, family preparation and participation in Holy Communion, the forgiveness and reconciliation of the sacrament of Holy Confession are, in practice, closely tied to the life of the family.

## Monogamy

The basic institution of the family is the idea of life-long monogamous marital bonds between one man and one woman. Anything which attacks that firm foundation, cuts away at the roots of our society. Yet, look at what is happening. Americans are becoming famous for "serial bigamy." The need for deep, long-lasting commitment between partners is being sidestepped with easy and frequent divorce patterns.

Orthodoxy has always recognized human frailty and has taken into consideration the need for divorce when, in fact, the marriage has ceased to exist. Yet, it has done this only with great difficulty and hesitation. Only Christian compassion motivates our church in sometimes granting ecclesiastical divorces. But that is a far cry from "no-fault divorce" "do it yourself divorces."

We have permitted our society to become patterned after the antics of Hollywood movie stars, for whom fifth, sixth and seventh marriages were common even during the forties and fifties. Increasing numbers of couples enter into marriage with the assumption that "if things don't work out. . . divorce is the easy solution." With such an attitude to begin with, how is it possible for differences to be resolved, for personalities to be honed to fit the process of mutual adjustment, so necessary for any lasting relationship? Our "throw away culture" has extended itself to include marriage as one of its "disposables."

## Sexual Faithfulness

The monogamous marriage, and especially the Christian marriage, is also based on the concept of sexual faithfulness. Under the moral principle of chastity is the exclusive sexual access which a husband and a wife reserve to their spouse. The Orthodox Church has always condemned the so-called "double standard" which demanded faithfulness of the wife, but allowed the husband to be promiscuous. This was always condemned as a violation of the marriage bond. As the sin of adultery, it is condemned as unworthy of the Christian life. Yet, our society "trumpets" the "affairs" of married persons as if they were no more significant than sharing a sandwich with a person of the opposite sex. Such behavior is often encouraged as "healthy" and as "liberating."

In the thirties such views were subsumed under the title "companiate marriage." Now it is called "open marriage." But the old name is just as good and much more accurate: adultery.

### Premarital Purity

We can see how far the moral standards of our society have degenerated when "conservative" President Ford's wife announced to all that she wouldn't be surprised if her own daughter was having an affair. It is true that Mrs. Ford did not explicitly advocate that unmarried persons should have premarital sexual relationships. But she did reflect the "Playboy standards of our times." What was shocking was not that she assumed that something like that could happen to her own daughter—every parent understands that—but that somehow it was really of no concern to her. An affair for an unmarried person was accepted quietly, without anxiety, concern or moral sensitivity. It was a "ho hum" type of activity of little significance or meaning. The message that it carried was reflective of our whole society: to speak of "premarital purity" is to make a joke. While birth control pills have encouraged young people to enter into all kinds of sexual relationships, venereal disease has become an epidemic among American young men and women.

The morality of the church, which sees the only proper exercise of sex as taking place within marriage, is clearly on the defensive. Though fornication has always existed in our society, this may be the first time that any recent society has actively encouraged it! Those of us who see this as a destructive development cannot help but deplore the erosion of our moral values and particularly warn our fellow citizens of the serious harm being done to the sanctity of marriage and the home.

## Parents and Children

Again and again studies have shown that the parent-child relationship is the most important factor in the life of an individual. School, church, peer group, television, music, movies, books, economics and many other factors influence the development of the child, but none is more significant than the relationship of parents to children. Yet, our society seems structured to weaken that relationship to a tenuous link. Most recently, laws have been passed in some states which do not require the permission or even the knowledge of parents for an abortion to be performed on their child.

Parents are brainwashed to think of their parenthood as something insignificant and of little import. Women are told that life has more in store for them than "mere motherhood." We would agree that motherhood is not the all-in-all for women. Yet to denigrate motherood in such a fashion seems to be one of the most sacreligious things a person can do.

In the place of respect for parents, television programs constantly present images of stupid, insensitive and careless fathers. The happy exceptions are few. The goal seems to be to separate parents and children as much as possible and for as long as possible. Young people are taught to "develop their individuality" as if personal development can take place only in antagonism betwen parents and children.

104

## The Consequences

The upshot of the situation is that with the family most of the important values of our nation are being lost. Problems of all kinds are being fomented in the process. When the family weakens, the whole of our society weakens. The faithfulness which makes monogamy possible is the same kind of attitude which makes the dependable worker, the dedicated professional and the committed soldier. As that fabric breaks down, it destroys the web of trust and dependence upon one another which permits social living.

The faithfulness which limits sexual relations to the marriage partner is cut from the same cloth which values loyalty, respect for personal integrity and honesty. As these disintegrate, so does the quality of life for all of us. As sex is cheapened to just selfish gratification and mutual exploitation, so life in general becomes tawdry, devoid of dignity and respect, itself a "cheap thrill," of little import and of great expendability.

The breakdown of parental authority and responsibility reflects a nation in which fewer and fewer of us sense the basic human responsibility we have for each other. Witness the heinous crimes perpetrated in every large city in our country, and the fear each has as he or she walks the street of every American metropolis.

## What Is Needed?

We need the restoration of family life. The old values must be recovered and put back into force. Commitment for life; mutual faithfulness of spouses; premarital purity; responsibility and respect in parent-child relationships; that is what is needed. It is needed now and in heavy application, if we are to save ourselves and this nation from decay and ultimate destruction.

The place to start is the home itself. Then the schools, the Church, the law as it is written and the law as it is interpreted in the courts must act courageously to turn the tide. In the last analysis what it requires is the recognition by all of us that one of the most sacred, fundamental and important institutions in the fabric of human society is the family. Commitment to that truth will generate its own corrections and reforms.

## 27. UNDERSTANDING MIXED MARRIAGES

This is a phenomenon well known to all of us. Many of our young people have entered into "mixed marriages." For them, the individual choice of a marriage partner because of love, outweighs the counsel of their elders. Fifty percent or more of the marriages performed in the Greek Orthodox Archdiocese of North and South America are mixed marriages.

We are often imprecise in the words which we use to describe this situation. Albert I. Gordon has written a book on the subject, providing us with a useful set of terms to describe some of the complexities. "Intermarriage" is applied in a general sense "to those married persons whose religious, racial or ethnic background is or was different from each other's, either prior to or after their marriage." If the partners retain their separate religious allegiances after their marriage, Gordon calls their marriage a "mixed marriage." Thus, if an Orthodox Christian marries a protestant their marriage is a mixed marriage. If, however, one of the partners converts to the religion of the other, it is called an intermarriage. Both cases, however, are "interfaith" marriages. If two people of different national backgrounds marry, theirs is an "interethnic" marriage. When persons of different racial backgrounds marry, there is an "interracial" marriage.

### Interfaith Marriage

How does the Orthodox Church view interfaith marriage? The church distinguishes between Christian and non-Christian interfaith marriages. It treats a marriage between an Orthodox Christian and a member of another Christian Church differently than it does when the non-Orthodox partner is Jewish, Moslem, Hindu, Buddhist, etc.

In the first case, the marriage of an Orthodox Christian to a non-Orthodox Christian (Roman Catholic, Episcopalian, Baptist, etc.), the Orthodox Church normally will sanctify the marriage. Orthodox Christians should know that they must be married in their own church if they are to remain in good standing with their church, that is, if they wish to continue to receive the sacraments in the Orthodox Church.

However, in the second case, in which an Orthodox Christian seeks to marry a non-Christian, the marriage cannot take place in the Orthodox Church. Thus, persons who enter into such marriages, in practice, excommunicate themselves.

## Interethnic Marriage

An intermarriage may be at once a mixed marriage religiously and interethnic as well. However, all interethnic marriages are not necessarily interfaith marriages. For instance if a Greek Orthodox Christian marries a Christian from the Antiochian, or Russian, or Bulgarian Orthodox Church, the marriage is interethnic, but not interfaith. Such a marriage is perfectly acceptable from a religious point of view. The ethnic and cultural differences may create problems for the couple, or may enrich their marriage, but from a strictly Orthodox Christian point of view the Orthodox Church has no hesitation to perform such a marriage.

## Interracial Marriage

Interracial marriage takes place when the partners belong to two different races, such as when a Caucasian and a

Negro marry. From the point of view of canon law, the Orthodox Church permits interracial marriages. Often, however, an interracial marriage is also an interfaith marriage. In that case, the rules and regulations covering interfaith marriages hold true. Thus, a white Orthodox Christian marrying an Asian Orthodox Christian, would be fully acceptable, canonically speaking. However, the marriage of a Caucasian Orthodox with a Negro Roman Catholic would require that the marriage take place in the Orthodox Church. A marriage between a Black Orthodox Christian and a Black Muslim could not be performed in the Orthodox Church.

### Pastoral Concerns

As you have seen, the church does not permit some kinds of intermarriages, according to its canon law. However, there is a pastoral dimension to all of these situations. This speaks not to rules and regualtions, but to the spiritual well-being and personal happiness of the faithful. The church does not encourage mixed marriages, in general.

Though it is true that many mixed marriages are successful, they often have more problems and difficulties than do those that take place between Orthodox Christians. That is why the church encourages the non-Orthodox Christian in such marriages to receive instruction and, if the non-Orthodox feels he or she can, become a member of the Orthodox Church. Many couples do this *before* they marry. Gordon writes: "marriages that commence as *mixed* marriages, where one of the partners has not formally accepted the religion of the other, are definitely less likely to 'work out'." For much of the same pastoral concern, interethnic and interracial marriages are not encouraged.

## 28. INTERFAITH MARRIAGES

For the Orthodox Church, the normal and desirable

marriage is between a man and a woman both of whom are practicing and faithful Orthodox Christians. The Sacrament unites persons of faith in a spiritual bond which joins them in life not only according to the flesh and emotions, but also spiritually. Together they pray, worship God, attend Church, participate in the Sacraments, fast and together they commune the Sacred and Holy Body of Christ in the Eucharist. Together they form a household and a family. Together they raise their children in the Church, baptising them and leading them to the Chalice. Together with their children they grow in the image of God. As a family they form "a Church in the home" (Romans 16:5, Philemon 2) and are a unified witness to the Orthodox faith and way of life.

### Early Attitudes

From the earliest times, however, this ideal situation has not always been realized among Christians. In the New Testament a person who become a Christian, but who previously was married to a non-Christian, was instructed not to abandon the unbelieving spouse because the unbelieving spouse would be sanctified by their union. However, if the unbelieving spouse wanted to dissolve the marriage that was acceptable (1 Corinthians 7:12-16). In general, the early Church disapproved of marriages of Orthodox Christians with Christian persons who were not members of the Orthodox Church (heretics) or with persons who were unbelievers (members of non-Christian religions).

There are a number of canons which express this position. For example, the 10th and 21st Canons of the Council of Laodicea (about 360 A.D.) counseled that marriages were not to take place between Orthodox and non-Orthodox Christians except if the non-Orthodox became Orthodox. A similar Canon of the 4th Ecumenical Council (451 A.D.) included in the prohibition of marriage with a "heretic, Jew, or Greek (pagan) unless they first promise and undertake to convert the person joined to the Orthodox Christian, to the Orthodox faith" (Canon 14).

## The Modern Situation

This strict rule has been modified somewhat in modern practice through the exercise of "economy" by the Church. According to current practice, an Orthodox Christian may marry a non-Orthodox Christian and remain in Sacramental communion with the Church if the non-Orthodox partner has been baptized in a Christian Church which believes in and baptizes persons in the name of the Holy Trinity, and if the marriage takes place with the Orthodox Sacrament of Matrimony. The Church would like to see the non-Orthodox become Orthodox, but since proselytizing is rejected, this is left to the free decision of the non-Orthodox spouse. If the marriage is not solemnized in the Orthodox Church, then the Orthodox partner is not in good Sacramental order with his or her Church and consequently may not participate in the rest of the Sacramental life of the Church. These persons consequently, may not receive Holy Communion or serve as sponsors at baptisms and weddings.

Marriages between Orthodox Christians and non-Orthodox persons, i.e., persons of other religions or of no faith (atheists, communists, etc.) are not permitted in the Orthodox Church according to present practice. Some concern however, about this situation has arisen in communist dominated countries and the forthcoming Great and Holy Council will address the issue. Generally speaking, however, the ancient Canons of the Church are enforced in this situation since the Sacrament of Marriage itself presupposes at minimum a conviction of faith in God as Holy Trinity and in Jesus Christ as Lord and Savior, and as Son of God. It is a question of debate whether the Church will also relax this ruling, but it does not seem likely that this will occur. The scriptural prohibition, "be not unequally yoked with unbelievers" (2 Corinthians 6:14) continues to be the policy of the Church. In practice, Orthodox Christians who marry non-Christians (Jew, Moslem, Hindu, Buddhist, member of a non-Christian sect, or one who has renounced the Christian faith for atheism or agnosticism), in effect excommunicate themselves.

This, together with all of the other considerations mentioned above cause the Church to strongly caution young people to be very careful in the choice of a spouse. The Church has never felt that chief considerations for a spouse should be physical beauty, wealth, social position or such factors. Young Orthodox people are urged by the Church to choose spouses from among the members of their own Church, and to seek out in the future marriage partner, nobility of spirit, Christian character, compatability of personality and culture. Were this to be more widely practiced, young people would find much less difficulty in their marriages. The ideal of the Orthodox Christian marriage remains the standard.

## Making It Work

However, when an inter-faith marriage does take place in the Orthodox Church, then both partners, their families and the Church must work and strive in extra measure to help make that marriage succeed. The couple themselves will need to resist the temptation to avoid inter-religious problems by avoiding religious practices altogether. Each will need to cultivate his or her religious life in order to be strengthened in character and spirit. The question of the upbringing of children is best addressed before they are born. Of course, the Orthodox Church expects and hopes that the children will be baptized and brought up in the Orthodox Church, but it does not make agreement to this a condition for performing the marriage. Partners in interfaith marriages will respect each other's traditions, values and sensitivities and will seek to maintain wholesome relationships with each other's families. Conversely, the families of young people who enter mixed marriages will seek to include the non-Orthodox spouse in the family group with love and care. Should the non-Orthodox spouse indicate interest in becoming an Orthodox Christian, family members will be encouraging but will never proselytize. Such decisions should be free and uncoerced. The Parish Priest and the Church as a whole need to pay special attention to inter-faith marriages, visiting and counseling the couple, encouraging their inclusion in the life and activities of the Parish wherever appropriate. Pastoral concern will also require that in pre- and post-marital counseling the non-Orthodox partner fully understands that marriage in the Orthodox Church neither makes him or her an Orthodox Christian, nor grants the privilege of participation in the Sacrament of Holy Communion or other Sacraments of the Orthodox Church. This instruction should be a part of a regular and standard pre-marital course of instruction, not only for planned mixed marriages, but for all persons marrying in the Orthodox Church.

## Non-Orthodox Marriages

When an Orthodox Christian has married outside the Orthodox Church to a spouse who has been baptized in another Christian Church, it is the responsibility of the Priest to carefully and sensitively seek to encourage the partners to have the Orthodox Sacrament of Marriage performed. Such marriages may take place quietly and without public attention. Pastoral discretion and care should be exercised so that unnecessary embarrassment be avoided, especially in cases of long-standing marriages.

The number of mixed marriages has rapidly increased in our Church in the past few years. This reflects a general pattern among most religious groups in our hemisphere. This phenomenon places an increased burden upon all involved, for the Church performs the Sacrament of Holy

Matrimony with the assumption of permanence. Statistical information indicates that inter-faith marriages have a higher rate of failure than do marriages where both partners are of the same faith, ethnic heritage, cultural background, social group, economic level, and educational achievement. If, in addition to religion, the other factors are also different, all persons involved including the Parish Priest, need to work together in the spirit of love, caring, mutual respect and special sensitivity to each other in order to help the marriage take root, grow and develop. The Lord said, "What God hath joined, let no man put asunder". This implies that we are all obligated to keep together with every possible means, that which God has joined. The Church performs each marriage, including the inter-faith marriage, with the intent that it fulfil its purposes and goals in a life-long, permanent union.

## 29. CHILD ABUSE

An apparently new social concern has risen in our days which highlights the abuse of children. Child abuse is generally understood in our day in broad terms, including the physical, mental, and spiritual harrassment of children. Specifically, child abuse is often understood as inflicting physical harm on children such as striking. punching, whipping, depriving them of physical needs, or subjecting them to sexual perversity. Also, included in the understanding of child abuse is the psychological and emotional harm caused by excessive criticism, denigration, constant verbal maltreatment, psychological abandonment, or hatred.

### Child Abuse in History
None of these evils, however, is new or unknown in history. In the period when Christianity first began to spread

throughout society, the place of children oftentimes was very precarious. Fathers had, in Roman Law, the right of life and death over their children. Abortion, infanticide, and the exposure of new born infants was a common practice. Young children who were exposed were frequently rescued by those who would use them for immoral purposes, such as pornography, homosexuality and prostitution. Christianity reacted strongly to these attacks against children and developed a widely-based and coherent moral teaching and practice reacting to wide-spread child abuse.

## The Heart of the Matter

At the heart of Christian teaching and moral values concerning child abuse is the whole Orthodox Christian understanding of marriage and family. One of the essential purposes of marriage is procreation. Spouses become parents not ony in a physical way, but also spiritual, since Orthodox Christianity understands procreation as the co-operation of husband and wife with God for the continuation of the human race not only in a physical sense but also morally and spiritually. For the Church, children are a gift from God who complete and fulfill the communion of husband and wife, in the image of the community of Divine Persons which is the Holy Trinity. Ethically, children are required to obey and respect their parents (Exodus 20:12) and parents assume the responsibility for the physical, moral and spiritual nurture of their children. The love of parents for their children is assumed by the teaching of the Church as natural and proper. It expresses itself in affection for children and concern for their welfare. Jesus asked, "If a son shall ask bread of any of you that is a father, will he give him a stone?", assuming the good will and intentions of the parent. The Church, expects as well, that parents will guide, direct, and discipline their children, including appropriate punishment when necessary. For, not to discipline offspring is to treat them "as illegitimate children, not as sons" (Hebrews 12:5-11). But discipline and punishment for the sake of correction must be motivated by love and genuine concern for the child, so the teaching of the Church also places limits: "Fathers, do not provoke your children to anger," (Ephesians 6:4) "lest they become discouraged" (Colossians 3:21). The major task of parents is to direct their children in the paths of the Lord, that they may know Him and in Christian faith, obedience, and Sacramental life, grow in the image of God toward Theosis. In addition, parents are obligated to educate and train their children to be good and useful members of society, to earn their living, so as to contribute to the general welfare and assist the poor and to develop a consciousness of service to humanity, as well as to prepare them in turn to become husbands, wives, and parents in the future.

## Abortion and Exposure

With this background, it becomes evident why very early in its history the Church sought to protect children from abuses of all kinds. Many of those early concerns are still pertinent today, and unfortunately, some new concerns have been added. The war against the child begins with abortion. What the Apologist Aristides said in the 2nd Century continues to be true today: "it is not permitted to destroy the fetus while it is still in the womb. . . . To prevent birth is to be beforehand with murder; and it makes no difference whether one kills a life already born, or suppresses it at birth. He is already a man who is about to be one; and every fruit already lives in its seed." (Apology IX, 6) Orthodox Christians will oppose abortion in principle and practice and will struggle to change the immoral legalization of abortion, as a legalization of murder.

Though exposure of children in a physical sense does not happen too often in our society, it still occurs elsewhere throughout the world. It should also be noted that moral, emotional and psychological abandonment is becoming more wide-spread among us. Morally, the ancient practice led to the sexual abuse of children. Justin Martyr, writing about the year 155 noted that Christians "hold it a crime to expose newborn infants . . . because we see that almost all of them are dragged into prostitution, not only the girls, but also boys . . . people raise adolescents for the sole purpose of abusing them obscenely" (1st Apology XXVII, 1). An alarming increase of child pornography, child prostitution and child homosexuality is now being reported in the press, and the Church must oppose it. Even more wide-spread in our society is the emotional abandonment of our children. Children are not "wanted", they are a "burden", it is not "fashionable" to have children. The neo-paganism of our times repeats the attitudes of the enemies of the child of every age. A pagan work called the "Satyricon" advised that one ought not to have children, for whoever does have any won't receive party invitations and won't be esteemed. In imitation, our day speaks of "mere motherhood" and denigrates parenthood, which the Church sees as cooperation with God. How can these be reconciled? Orthodox Christians in precept, word and deed will affirm both parenthood and childhood.

### Abandonment

Another concern unique to our time, is that children are isolated from the rest of the social fabric with their own music, styles, values, heroes, etc. Among the chief culprits in this "abandonment" is television. Parents use TV today to "baby sit" their children. But it has taken over the family. The Greek Orthodox Archdiocese Department of Religious Education pamphlet on TV refers to "the way the TV subtly gets control of our lives . . . TV casts out the natural experiences of the family, the daily give and take, the conversations and the personal sharing . . . It reshapes family life. It influences the raising and growth of children. It shapes and molds people's attitudes and world view almost without their realizing it." (*Television in the Christian Home, p.5*).

This psychological abandonment of our children allows all sorts of un-Christian values to enter the hearts and minds of our children, something no Christian parent may properly do. For it is the responsibility of parents to nurture, educate, and guide their child in the ways of faith, moral values, and spiritual life. A Christian writing from the earliest period of the Church instructs Christian parents "Do not neglect your son or daughter; but teach them from childhood the fear of God." (Didache IV, 9). It is abuse of of our children to permit the secular society to imbue them with materialistic, secularist and immoral values, denying to them the "waters of life" (Revelation 21:6) which come from God, for we deny to them in fact, their true light and life" (John 1:4; 11:25, 20:31). What greater abuse can there be! We must support all efforts of the Church, movements in society and civil efforts to provide a spiritually and morally wholesome environment for our children and wage a vigorous struggle against all that pollutes and distorts their lives, what ever form it may take.

### Drug and Bodily Abuse

One of the greatest abuses of children is the diabolical spread of drugs. Young people are systematically introduced to various drugs and made psychologically and physically dependent upon them. This fearsome addiction attacks their whole being, destroying their moral freedom and spiritual growth. If abuse of alcohol is condemned by the Church (Romans 13:13, Galatians 5:21), how much more so does the Orthodox Church oppose involvement with illicit drugs? As a Church we are unalterably opposed to drug use by our own people, with special concern for our children, as well as all persons in our society. As a Church we support efforts by our government in its war against the traffikers in drugs.

It remains, to be noted that the Orthodox Church utterly condemns those who physically do bodily harm to children. Children are to be treated with love, concern, patience, and understanding. The tenderness of Jesus toward children is the source of our opposition to child abuse. "And He took a child, and put him in the midst of them; and taking him in his arms, he said to them, 'Whoever receives one such child in my name, receives me; and whoever receives me, receives not me, but him who sent me'" (Mark 9:36-37). Thus, the remarkable conclusion: to treat a child with love is to show love for God. But the opposite is fearsome: to abuse a child is to abuse God!

## 30. DIVORCE: ITS MAJOR CAUSE

Everyone knows that the divorce rate is skyrocketing. Depending upon which authority you read, one in every four or one in every three marriages ends up on divorce. In California the rate of divorce is higher. In a small town or city in the deep South it is likely that the rate drops. But wherever you are, it is almost impossible to be in contact with people and not count at least a few of your friends or acquaintances who have been divorced once, and perhaps even twice.

### What Causes Divorces?

The reasons, it is honest to say, are myriad. Each couple that goes through the terrible ordeal of a divorce has their own unique answer to the question. Some say it is sexual: poorly informed couples break up because of their inability to maintain a harmonious and pleasing sexual relationship. Another reason frequently given is the immaturity of younger couples: "They just weren't ready to get married," we say. Money is another often given reason: either disparate financial backgrounds or too little of it, are special cases noted. Others point to the lack of proper education for marriage and family living. Many point to the incompatibility of personalities as a major cause.

In truth, all or none of the above may be a cause of divorce in a specific case, and all of them surely have been the cause of some divorces. The lists could be expanded infinitely: social pressures, business reverses, religiously mixed marriages, ethnically mixed marriages, racially mixed marriages, in-law interference, in-law indifference, etc. So it would in practice be quite foolish to single out one cause for divorce in our times. Yet, there is one general phenomenon which certainly can be lifted up for particular attention as a cause for the serious divorce rate which our nation faces.

## One Major Cause

*Newsweek* magazine once had a feature article on the family. It pointed out the obvious: that the family in America is having a rough time of it. It was not only the divorce statistics, it was also the examination of the changes taking place within the family. One of the important changes was the tendency of all members of the family to go their own ways.

The scene is quite familiar. On any given night, father sits in front of the TV set, mother is at a committee meeting, eldest son is on a date, high school daughter is doing homework with a friend, and the youngest child is listening to a night baseball game with his own radio and ear-set. It is not that these activities are evil in themselves. But when they are taken collectively and multiplied by evening after evening, they affect the very stuff out of which family life is made.

The disintegration of the family unit does not begin, advance and fullfill itself without a powerful ally: preoccupation with the self and its satisfaction and service. Our society has taken a normal, healthy and responsible concern for one's self and turned it into a destructive and ugly motive for all of our action.

Preoccupation with what pleases *us*, what satisfies *us*, with "our thing," is the order of the day. Youngsters are taught the "gimmies" from the moment they watch their first TV commercial. Students are instructed by school and peer group to hate discipline and self-control and to celebrate the fulfillment of their own wants. "Me-myself-and I" become the three most frequently used words in our vocabulary. The consumerism of the economic system becomes the rule of thinking. "What's in it for me?" becomes the most important question to ask before making any kind of decision.

### What a Good Marriage Demands

It may seem that we have gone afar from our topic. But that is not the case. The selfish egoistic, "me-first" attitude of our age plays a large role in promoting divorce. A good marriage demands, above all, just the opposite of what was described above. Marriages survive and grow rich in meaning when each of the partners give consideration *first* to their spouse.

Marriage means not only that a man and a woman are joined together, but that they are help-mates, one to another. Marriage means that each partner cherishes the other and is concerned for the welfare of the partner. In sexual relations, love also means thought and feeling for the partner. In financial matters, understanding, flexibility and sensitivity to the wants and needs of the spouse. In young marriages, it is learning quickly to put the partners first, and the self second. Even incompatible personalities can succeed in marriage, if mutual regard and concern replace self-regard and selfishness. Mixed marriages, whether religious, ethnic or racial can and do succeed if self-cenderedness is abandoned and mutuality of love replaces it as the chief motivation in married life.

A good marriage demands love of each partner. And love means that you place another in the center of your own life. Our Lord taught us that to love God meant having God in our hearts, our souls, our minds and our whole strength. A good marriage means that the husband concerns himself in his heart, his mind, his soul and his body with the well-being of his wife; and that the wife concerns herself in heart, soul, mind and strength with the well-being of her husband. A good marriage learns to minimize selfishness and preoccupation with the self.

In a good marriage there is continuing appreciation, respect, reverence and love of the partners for each other. A good marriage binds husband and wife closer together, so that in a sense there is a blurring of personalities. The husband learns from his wife and takes upon himself some of her finer characteristics. And the wife loses a bit of herself in her husband while gaining something from him for herself.

### How Not to Have a Divorce

You can protect yourself and your spouse from any thought of divorce by constantly reminding yourself that precoccupation with your wishes, your desires, your wants alone are sure paths to the divorce court. Put your spouse first in your marital relationship. Love him or her. That is, do whatever you can which is for *his* or *her* well-being and benefit. Of course, if husband and wife act in this fashion, something very impressive happens: instead of selfishly grasping at their own well-being the spouses provide that well-being for each other!

Yes, one of the major causes of divorce is the widespread cult of self which is so dominant in our country. But people are beginning to see how destuctive it is. They are affirming once again the precious truth of God that "love . . . never fails" (1 Corinthians 13:5, 8). If preoccupation with self is one of the major causes of divorce, then it can be said with certainty that divorce is avoided and marriage is strengthened when selfishness is replaced by genuine love, that is, with mutual heartfelt concern for the welfare of our partner in marriage.

# Part IV

# SOCIAL ISSUES

## 31. DO POLITICS BECOME THE CHRISTIAN?

"Render unto Caesar what is Caesar's and unto God, what is God's" is a teaching of Christ. From one perspective it means at least that Christ saw the Church as something very different from the State and its methods.

Yet, "Render unto Caesar, that which is Caesar's" is also a command. It seems to imply that there is a responsibility to be exercised toward the State by the Church, too. How is this to be explained?

While we can think of the church as *official*, we also know that the church is the body of the believers who have been baptized in the name of the Holy Trinity and who live the sacramental life. When we think of it that way, every Christian helps make up the church and few of us would agree that it is right for the whole body of the faithful to stay out of politics, even partisan politics. The reason for this is that we do have a duty to "render unto Casear, that which is Caesar's."

### Christian Citizenship

Politics isn't only voting for candidates for public office. The ancient Greeks understood *politics* as the art of governing. In a democracy that means that the people share in the governing process. And *that* means that Christians are of necessity involved in politics. That is the point. Should the Christians who make up the church help govern the city and county and state and nation in which they live? Or to put it in other words, is there such a thing as Christian citizenship?

Well, the early Christians certainly acted as if there

was. The first thing they did was to make sure that they obeyed the laws. The New Testament makes a point of that. They also took advantage of the protection provided by "due process." Saint Paul appealed to the Emperor as a Roman citizen when he felt he had an unfair trial. The early Christian writers, known as the Apologists, wrote letters to the Emperor to express their views on what they felt was an unjust law (the persecution of Christians).

Later on in the Church's history, countless patriarchs, bishops, clergy and laypersons worked in the political system of Byzantium for laws which embodied Christian values. For example, laws regarding the status of women, the protection of infants and children, the improvement of the condition of slaves, and the treatment of the poor, became concerns of the church.

### Involvement Necessary for Christians

In a democracy such as ours, *Orthodox Christians* are called upon to continue that tradition. Individual Orthodox Christians will study the issues, examine the records of candidates and vote regularly. Some will be convinced that they should support the campaigns of some candidates. Others will run for public office themselves.

The important thing is that we participate in the political enterprise as Christians, as members of the church. And lest I be misunderstood, let me add that Christians should not become involved in politics for self-serving purposes, but in order to serve justice, to enhance citizenship, to do good works before all people and on behalf of all people. If, as some say, "politics is a dirty business," then Christians will seek to clean it up and to help it fulfill its real purpose.

The church is properly involved in politics when her members participate in the electoral process, write letters of Christian opinion to their elected representatives, join a political party, express their Christian opinion in public forum and work in groups seeking to improve the condition of public life. Further, they are involved in politics when they pray daily and on Sundays, as we do in the Divine Liturgy, for the civil rulers of our nation, for peace, for the cities in which we live, etc.

In answer to the title question "Do Politics Become the Christian?" the response is plain. In a society such as ours, in order to render unto Caesar that which is his, Orthodox Christians necessarily will be involved in politics. Being involved in politics is part of what it means to be a Christian.

## 32. A NATION IN CRISIS

Over the past decade or so America has been rocked by the revelation of evil in high places, on the national as well as the state levels. The scandal of an American Vice-President resigning from office as a result of serious bribery charges would have been enough. But the political chicanery of Watergate; the unrelieved cynicism of the tapes; the huge public expenditures on private property; the "final and complete" explanations which became "inoperative" within a few days; followed finally by the first resignation of a President of the United States, all flowed together into a torrent of moral impropriety which has shattered the nation's confidence in our elected leadership.

Nearly every state in the nation has had its prosecution of graft-grabbing politicians, under-the-table deals, and mafia executions.

Without question, the average, decent people of the country have had enough. They will be the first to admit that no one is perfect and no one is guiltless before the sinless God. Yet, the serious revelations of the recent years have stripped the average citizen of that mantle of tolerance for human frailty.

Decent people, quite reluctantly, have begun to accept

128

the fact that dishonesty, duplicity and distrust dominate much of the highest levels of government.

## The New Situation

With the change of public leadership, the exposé of the press and other media, the homey and likeable personalities of the presidents who followed Watergate, it appears that the people of the nation have turned their attention away from the moral quality of our public life to the bread and butter issues of inflation, jobs, recession and taxes.

Yet, the issue of the moral status of our nation will not be dismissed so easily. We may pretend that new faces have caused it to disappear. We may no longer fret about it and discuss it as frequently. However, it would be wise for the people of our nation not to get drowsy over the issue of public morality because serious things have been happening to us. What has happened is a fundamental and radical change in the American public ethic which made possible the blatant and hidden corruption of these past few years.

## Old Values—New Values

It is the thesis of some students of Greek Orthodox immigration to the United States that the Greek immigrants brought with them certain values which fit very well with the dominant values of America during the first half of the century. And for this reason, it is argued, the Greek-Americans succeeded so spectacularly in comparison with other immigrant groups.

Foremost was the sense of personal self-respect and dignity. In Greek, it was called *philotimo*. It meant a commitment to personal character and integrity. Nothing was more to be protected than a good name. This led directly to a sense of responsible membership in the community. It meant willingly and happily taking up responsibility together with others for the general well-being of all. It also meant a pride in one's country. Greeks found it easy to expand their patriotic feelings about their homeland to include their adopted country.

The Greek-American Orthodox Christians did not have to be prodded to work. They enjoyed their work and their mentality fit very well with the dominant view that hard work and frugality were the virtues that led to success. And frugal they were. They were careful how they spent their resources. Their money went for the basics: good food, respectable clothing, a decent house. They knew how to postpone satisfying their desires—they were no example for the consumer society! Pleasures, too, were limited to the family and church community. Though they might own a fancy restaurant or even a night-club, their own recreation was modest, restrained and far from hedonistic. And finally, they had deep communal religious feelings which were expressed at their Orthodox Church, which they quickly chose to call their "community."

These values found almost mirror images in the dominant patterns: self-respect, responsible citizenship, patriotism, willingness to work, frugality, family and home, as well as deep religious feeling. They characterized Greek immigrants and their heritage; they characterized the America to which they came.

## The American Moral Crisis
The political events of the past few years reflect a substantial change in the moral situation in America. The old values are under attack. It is difficult even to explain *philotimo* today. How could anyone ever place a sense of dignity and self-respect before immediate advantage and the desire of the moment? "Do your own thing" tends to supplant the sense of community responsibility. No sophisticate is patriotic any more. "Labor-saving" . . . "the four day week" . . . "sloppy workmanship" . . . are today's mottos.

The consumer society, fostered by the principle of "instant gratification," is dominant, while conservationists and opponents of deficit spending fight the uphill battle. And finally, we are living through days when the two fundamental building blocks of any well-ordered society, the family and the church, are under severe and unrelenting attack. We are a nation which has turned around and upon itself and is in the process of devouring its own lifeblood.

### The Answer

There is an answer. It is one of repentance (a "changing of the mind"). As naive and preposterous as it may sound, we must find the ways to revivify and revitalize those values which underpin the greatness of this nation. Watergate was a mere episode in the light of what may yet happen to our nation. Repentance must happen. That it can happen was seen in the curious phenomenon of the temporary disappearance of the generation-gap when young people listened in awe, admiration and approval to Senator Sam Ervin quote Scripture, the Constitution and Shakespeare in defense of the traditional American values during the Watergate trials.

The moral crisis in America is not over. We deceive ourselves if we believe that. A crisis, however, is a turning point. Orthodox Christians may perhaps be making their greatest contribution to America by contributing to the direction in which that crisis will move by simply remaining true to themselves and to their own heritage.

## 33. HUMAN RIGHTS

In the tradition of the Bible and the Church, the great emphasis in moral teaching has been upon our duties toward others. There is little in the sources of our Faith which highlight and emphasize claims for the fulfillment of rights. Yet, every duty is, in fact, a response to a morally just and correct claim upon our behavior by another, that is, a right. Consequently, each person has both duties and rights. As a result Christians have always accorded moral human rights to all people. Basic human rights are founded on the theological truth that all persons are created in the image and likeness of God, and consequently, every human being has an inviolate dignity as a child of God who, just because he or she exists, has claims upon the behavior of others persons toward them.

Further, just as human rights have meaning only in relationship to others, in the same manner individual human rights cannot be thought of except as woven together with the rights of others, which are oftentimes expressed, not as the rights of individuals only but also of groups, peoples and nations. Human rights are so fundamental to our human condition that they are not abrogated even when it is accepted that we are all imperfect and sinful as persons and as social groups. Human rights reside in us as witnesses to the irreducible dignity which we have as creatures created in the image and likeness of God.

## Recent Statements

Orthodox Christians will not emphasize these rights over the equally significant duties and requirements which we have as children of God but neither are we entitled to ignore or depricate them either for ourselves or for others. Consequently, our Church clearly speaks in defense of genuine human rights which are applicable to all peoples. In recent years, for example, under the leadership of Archbishop Iakovos, we have expressed concern about the violation of the rights of our fellow Greek Orthodox Christians in Turkey and Cyprus before the public, the White House, and the United Nations. But the Church's concern has not been limited to its own. Both the Archbishop and the Clergy Laity Congresses of the Greek Orthodox Archdiocese have made appeals for the human rights of many and varied suffering persons and groups in the past. In addition, there has been a steady effort to raise the consciousness of the Church and those outside the Church regarding human rights in general. Characteristic is this passage from a 1971 Encyclical of Archbishop Iakovos:

> *By the term, "dignity of man", no outward and frivolous niceties are implied. Man's need for dignity springs from the very essence of his being.*
>
> *Dignity is the essence of life itself and from it alone is derived the right of man to call himself son of God. Not one of the institutions of man can stand alone without it; whether it be the family, society, the Church, education, or civilization itself. Institutions are to serve people but if they do not help the individual to be free and to remain free and self-respecting, to feel that he is truly the son of God, the brother and an equal to all others, they do not serve their own purpose. Exploitation, discrimination, social injustice all are those indominable forces, characteristic of, but which inevitably bring about the downfall of the reign of the rulers of the darkness of this age.*

Statements on human rights were also adopted by the Clergy-Laity Congresses of the Greek Orthodox Archdiocese in 1966 (18th Clergy-Laity), 1968 (19th Clergy-Laity), and 1970 (20th Clergy-Laity) and in 1978 (24th Clergy-Laity). In addition, the 1964 Clergy-Laity affirmed and adopted as its own a statement on Civil Rights. Another statement, observing the thirtieth anniversary of the Universal Declaration of Human Rights by the United Nations was issued by SCOBA in December 1978. Included in this statement, which was affirmed by a special communication of the Greek Orthodox Archdiocese, was this paragraph:

> *We urge all Orthodox Christians to mark this occasion with prayers for those whose human rights are being denied and/or violated; for those who are harassed and persecuted because of their religious be-*

*liefs, Orthodox and non-Orthodox alike, in many parts of the world; for those whose rightful demands and persistance are met with greater oppression and ignominy; and for those whose agony for justice, food, shelter, health care and education is accelerated with each passing day.*

*We ask that you support President Carter's request that the Senate approve the United Nations International Covenants on Economic, Social and Cultural Rights, and on Civil and Political Rights, as recorded in the Universal Declaration of Human Rights.*

The list of particular human rights in this SCOBA statement serves to illustrate, but it does not exhaust, these rights. It is difficult to adequately enumerate and list every right appropriate to human beings as human beings created in the image and likeness of God. Among the most basic and fundamental, from the point of view of the Church, are the following: life and dignity, liberty, basic needs, and equality.

The human rights begin with the right to our life. No other rights can be enjoyed if the right to life is not respected. This right is universally acknowledged, but widely violated. Innocent victims of crime, political oppression, exploitation, the arms race, legalized abortion, racial violence, excessive nationalism and all forms of injustice are mute witnesses to the widespread violation of this right. An extension of this right is the need to accord to human beings and human associations a fundamental recognition of their inherent dignity. Respecting the humanity in each of us with tolerance and forebearance (Ephesians 4:2) especially when we do not understand, agree with or accept the views of the other is a far from realized practice. Ethnic hatred, racial prejudice, class stereotypes, commercial irresponsibility, political extremisms constantly serve to violate this common right to be accorded human dignity.

## A Theology of Human Rights
In Orthodox theology, the *autexousion,* that is, the self-determining ability is an essential part of our humanity. To deny human beings freedom is to deny to them an essential part of the humanity with which God has endowed them. The human right of liberty and freedom expresses itself in many ways. Individually it means that persons are entitled to basic civil and political rights which are extensions of the fundamental capacity of self-determination which we have as human beings. These rights are expressed both individually and as peoples. Consequently the right to free association and to national self-determination belong to all. For the Church, a chief and primary right is the right of full religious freedom, including worship, teaching and mission.

## Identifying Human Rights
In our times, however, all of these rights are systematically trampled upon. Totalitarian regimes in both hemispheres stamp out the right to liberty and freedom repeatedly and in every conceivable manner.

There are basic needs, which must be met if human life is to achieve any measure of its potential. Life and freedom are the first of these. But a measure of economic resources is also necessary to provide adequate food, housing, health care and education for a useful life in society. The duty of each person to work, meeting at once the needs of others through the service of our labor, as well as the basic needs of our own lives and of those dependent upon us (2 Thessalonians 3:10) is at once a right to be claimed. Yet the world structures under which we live deny to the vast majority of the earth's population access to enough food, clothing, housing, health care and education, while overindulging certain select societies with a surplus of these. And within each of these societies excessive inequalities permit, for example, some to starve, while others grow fat in a surfeit of waste.

Such injustice attacks another basic human right— the right to equal treatment in reference to basic human rights themselves. Equality does not mean the leveling of every talent, ability, reward, or honor. Equality cannot mean the elimination of all human social distinctions for this flies in the face of the right of freedom. Nor does equality mean that individuals or groups may with impunity tear up the moral and social fiber of human life. It does mean, however, that the basic human rights which all persons and groups are entitled to may not be denied to persons or groups arbitrarily or for discriminatory reasons. Racial prejudice and the denial of human dignity for women as practiced in many, if not all of the nations of the world, are examples of the denial of this right to equal treatment.

This listing of human rights is not exhaustive. Each of those mentioned can be developed in more detail. For example, in the area of civil and political human rights we may note many violations such as the proliferation of political prisoners, the widespread incidence of political refugees, the increase of politically motivated "disappearances," torture, assassinations, terrorism, hostage taking, private military and para-military groups, detention without trial, farcical "show" trials without genuine and fair due process, forced hospitalization in mental institutions, deportations, exile, arbitrarily imposed death sentences and efforts at genocide. All these violate fundamental human rights.

## Defending Human Rights

Though it will be impossible by mere human efforts to stop the violation of human rights since both as persons and societies we are sinful, imperfect, incomplete and distorted, this does not mean that we may content ourselves with pronouncements and rhetoric. Consciousness and sensitivity to the human rights of others is a virtue exemplified by the Old Testament prophets and by Jesus Christ Himself. It is particularly easy for us to be sensitive to the violations of our own rights and the rights of those close to us, but to systematically ignore the violations of the rights of others, especially if we are the perpetrators of these violations. Awareness, though important *and* difficult, is not enough. We must act. Frequently Archbishop Iakovos has charged the Church through his encyclicals, to act on specific issues. The 1978 SCOBA Human Rights statement concluded with appeals to action. Yet, in most cases we remain passive and uninvolved. However, on occasion we have shown that we can act in concert, as a people and as a Church. The effective reaction to the Cyprus crisis by the whole Greek Orthodox Archdiocese is a case in point. We need to develop just as effective concern and action in other areas of human rights, as well. As the SCOBA declaration says, we need "a new awareness and a renewed dedication and commitment to Human Rights, as the God-given inalienable rights for all His people".

## 34. EQUAL RIGHTS

Because of our creation in the image and likeness of God, all human beings have fundamental, inalienable human rights. Among these are the rights to life, dignity, liberty, basic needs—such as food, housing, health care and education, and equality, as seen in the preceeding.

Equal rights refers to equal access and treatment in regard to basic rights such as those mentioned above. It cannot and does not mean the leveling of all human distinctions, all human reward, and all human achievement since these are dependent as well upon many other factors such as individual and personal characteristics, as well as one's own self-determination. Yet prejudice, unfair laws and discriminatory practices often deny to persons rights which are due them as human beings. The Church is concerned with the righting of these injustices.

Two of the most widespread groups subject to the denial of equal rights are racial minorities and women. Increasingly, persons identified with practices traditionally held to be immoral are demanding a recognition of equal rights, as well, such as those who practice homosexuality, lesbianism, prostitution and pornography.

## Racial Equality

The Orthodox Church, generally speaking, does not have a history of racial prejudice, since from the very beginning it has been "catholic," that is, a Church composed of many peoples, nations and races. From the earliest times the Church has included in its membership persons of all colors. In our own day indigenous churches of Caucasians, Blacks, and Asians share the common chalice. In the Greek Orthodox Archdiocese during the last decade and a half, we have seen many instances of concern with racial issues. In 1964 the Standing Conference of Canonical Orthodox Bishops under Archbishop Iakovos issued a statement on racial justice, which was endorsed by the Clergy-Laity Conference of the Greek Orthodox Archdiocese of that same year. Calling upon a shared history of persecution, the resolution joined the Church "with our fellow Christians and citizens everywhere in deploring all vestiges of segregation that deny to free men the dignity of equal rights." (*The 15th Clergy-Laity Congress: Resolutions Adopted,* N.Y., 1960, pp. 17-29). The next year Archbishop Iakovos marched in Selma in a show of solidarity in the struggle for equal rights in our nation. The Archbishop referred to the racial issues repeated in encyclicals over the following years and in the Keynote Addresses of the 18th (1966), the 20th (1970) and the 22nd (1974) Clergy-Laity Congresses. The Clergy-Laity Congresses themselves have made frequent mention of the issue, the 20th (1970) and the 21st (1972) having issued long statements on the subject. The latter called for

> *support (of) efforts which will assure equal educa-
> tion, equal employment, open housing and equal op-
> portunities for human development in general to
> people of color from whom they have been denied in the
> past. The conscience of America can no longer tolerate
> injustices registered against others simply because
> their skin pigmentation happens to be something other
> than white. Racial hatred and prejudice, expressed
> most overtly in the past against the American Indians,
> the Blacks and the Chicanos contradict the Gospel of
> Christian love which proclaims that in Jesus Christ
> there is neither Jew nor Greek, slave nor free, male
> nor female. (Report of the Social and Moral Issues
> Committee, Decisions of the 21st Clergy-Laity Con-
> gress. N.Y., 1972, pp. 67-68.)*

Yet many Orthodox Christians have adopted from the
society around us and maintain, isolated from their Christian convictions, commonly held attitudes of racial prejudice. The pronouncements of the Church need to be made
personal convictions of our members and as Church people
we must change both our attitudes and our actions to conform with those teachings. As children of God, we cannot
deny to our brothers the equal rights due them. More will
be said about this below.

### Equal Rights for Women

The question of equal rights for women is a flaming
issue in our times. Historically, the issue is complicated
because of the profound effect of this question on the structures of society and the family. On the one hand, it is possible to trace through the history of the Church a change in
attitude about women as compared to ancient practices. It
was Christianity which recognized the fundamental
equality of the sexes before God in His teaching. Orthodox
Christian doctrine permits no qualitative differentiation
between men and women in their essential humanity.
Women, according to Orthodox Christian beliefs, may not

be considered inferior beings and must be accorded rights due every human being. Thus any laws, practices, prejudices, social or cultural traditions which deny to women life, dignity, liberty, basic needs and equal access to them are to be condemned as unchristian. A current issue which the Orthodox Church faces in the United States today is the proposed Equal Rights Amendment to the Constitution.This proposed amendment has caused much controversy. Its advocacy by strident and extremist women's liberation movement groups, on the one hand, and its passionate condemnation by those who oppose it create an atmosphere where understanding from an orthodox perspective is needed. The opponents to ERA argue that its passage will cause the break down of the family, result in combat duty for women, unisex public toilet facilities, and grant constitutional legitimacy to homosexuality and sexual perversion. It is safe to say that the Orthodox Church is opposed to all of these, and considers it part of its faith and practice to strengthen all those forces which support the biblically-based traditional morality on these subjects. Yet, it is not at all clear or provable that the predicted consequences of the Equal Rights Amendment necessarily will follow. The proposed amendment is very brief: "Equality of rights under the law shall not be denied or abridged by the United States or any state on account of sex." This is followed by two enabling clauses authorizing appropriate legislation and setting the time of its implementation. From the position of the doctrine and belief of the Orthodox Church it seems impossible that the opposite of what is said in the proposed amendment could be supported by Orthodox Christians. Whether, however, the Church will want to politically lobby for the Equal Rights Amendment is questionable. Part of the unwillingness of Orthodox Church members to do so is related to some associated issues. Even so, it should be clear that support for the equal application of the laws of the land to all persons of both sexes does not mean that we ignore the significant and important roles in the Church and society which are unique to women. This is based on women's God given role and task as mother. Nothing in the ERA can properly be construed as undermining the high privilege, dignity and honor which women alone have to give birth to, nurture and morally and spiritually guide the future generations. No employment, no matter how lucrative, powerful, influential or creative can supercede in value the conscientious and responsible giving of life and nurture to a human being. When the mother is a Christian who cooperates with God in the making of new human beings and incorporating them in the Kingdom of God through His Church, there is no greater dignity and honor. Women are due equal rights as persons—yet, their special role and calling transcends such legal formulations. We would quarrel strenuously with those who would minimize, denigrate and weaken the unique and lofty calling of women in their roles as wives, mothers and homemakers.

## Other Claims

We hold that the rights of which we speak are essential human rights, which may not be denied to any human being. They are the fundamental rights which pertain to every person, good or bad, moral or immoral, saint or sinner. Persons who identify themselves variously as homosexuals, lesbians, prostitutes and pornographers also demand the right to life, human respect, political freedom, the basic needs for life and equal treatment regarding these persons. For, regardless of how it judges their activities, the spirit of Jesus Christ who recognized the essential human values of even the greatest of sinners (John 8:7, Matthew 9:10-11, Mark 2:17, Luke 7:34) leads the Church to a fundamental respect for the humanity of all persons. But the Church opposes vehemently laws and practices which, instead of curtailing and limiting practices destructive to the fabric of society, contributes to its dissolution. The Church will never accede to supposed rights of individuals to the legalization of so-called "alternative life styles" and supposed rights of persons to weaken and attack the institutions of marriage and the family. Basic human rights for all persons must be honored and protected but acts of moral perversity may not be properly accorded that dignity.

## 35. ARE ORTHODOX CHRISTIANS RACIST?

Americans, of all backgrounds have become much more sensitive to the charge that we are a racist society, and that those who make up our society are imbued with the spirit of racism. Orthodox Christians would do well to ask themselves how true this charge is of us; whether in theory or in practice we are racist, and if so, what our reaction to this should be.

Very strictly speaking, distinctions of race are not simply in terms of color or skin and other similar characteristics. *Race* refers to the descendants of a common ancestor; a family, tribe, people or nation, believed to belong to the same stock. *Racism* is the belief that some races or a race is by nature superior to others, and consequently discriminating against the "lesser" races and justifying "special privileges" for the "superior" race.

As defined above, it is clear that the existence of races is an inevitable fact. The word is defined so flexibly so that any group may be called a race. In the context of the charge that our nation is a racist society, it refers to the very obvious groupings of skin color separating Caucasian peoples whose skin is pinkish-white from all other people whose skin is dark, ranging from light brown to black.

### The Teaching of the Church
The Holy Orthodox Church recognizes the fact of race. There are all kinds of groups which may bear the name of

142

race, including what is often called the "white race" and
the "black race." In the view of the church it is in God's design that there be social, ethnic, national and physical
races. He has created a world of much variety, many hues
and infinite differences. The question, then, is not one of
whether such variety is good, since God created His world
"and saw that it was good." Our theologians emphasize,
however, that in the story regarding the creation of man,
the Bible stresses the ultimate common origin and fundamental unity of all mankind.

In the eyes of the church, all peoples, regardless of the
groupings into which they fall, share in the common heritage of two fundamental characteristics. First, as we have
noted, all people share in the common heritage of their
creation by God in His image and in His likeness. In this
we are all sons and daughters of our heavenly Father; and,
consequently, naturally brothers and sisters to each other.

The second common heritage, which all men and wom-
en and all people of every race share in, is our common sin-
fulness. *All* of us have need of forgiveness, restoration,
communication with God and sanctification. *All* of us continuously fall short of the goals for which God has created
us. *All* of us sin.

### Are We Racist?

In this most vital dimension of our lives, then, we find it
easy to fall into attitudes, practices and actions which witness to our failure to be the kind of people we were created
to be. One of these sins is pride, the kind of pride which expresses itself in the prejudiced attitudes of racism. There is
no doubt that we Greek Orthodox Christians continuously
violate the principles of our faith with racist attitudes.

The Ecumenical Patriarchate in the relatively recent
past condemned this view as the sin of "phyletism". It
based its teaching on sound biblical and patristic tradition.
There is a difference between reasonable pride in one's own

group, race, nation or people, and the racist assumption of the superiority of one's own group. However, we do the latter continuously. If we examine ourselves carefully, we will no doubt find many examples of racism in our thinking, our speaking, our attitudes and our behavior.

### What Can We Do?

Repentence means "change of mind". That is the first order of business for Christians who would free themselves from the sin of racist pride. That change can come about only when we begin to see people of other groups and colors as fellow children of the same heavenly Father, as genuine brothers and sisters under God, and as fellow seekers of true humanity in Jesus Christ. *That* can become real when we seek to change our own attitudes, to support all efforts at erasing prejudicial treatment against unfairly treated groups. In doing that, we practice the virtue of Christian love, for we seek the welfare of our brother in so doing.

Propagating the Christian faith in the society in which we live will also help us to erase the sin of racism from our lives, because it will constantly keep before us our common divine heritage, our common human need for redemption and our common destiny to realize our full humanity as the image and likeness of God.

## 36. THE SUPREME COURT ABORTION DECISION

On January 22, 1973, the Supreme Court of the United States made its long awaited ruling on abortion. It declared in a 7 to 2 vote that during the first three months of pregnancy the decision to have an abortion should be left entirely to the woman and her doctor. During the next three months the state's interest in the health of the mother and in the life of the unborn child is great enough to permit standards and conditions to be set under which abortions may or may not take place. In the last three month period a state may, if it chooses, prohibit all abortions, except those required to save the life of the mother. These restrictions on the freedom to perform abortions are based on the state's constitutional responsibility to protect the life of its citizens.

## The Reasons Given

Justice Harry A. Blackmun, who wrote the majority decision, used two basic lines of reasoning to justify the decision. The first was the Constitution's mention of personal liberty. This was broadened to include a woman's decision to bear a child or not. The Supreme Court thus adopted the view that the fetus, during the first three months was not a person and not in any way protected by the law.

However, the second line of thinking indicated that at a certain point in time—the beginning of the fourth month—"the potential life of the unborn infant becomes sufficient to justify some state regulation of abortion." And further,—at the beginning of the seventh month—states may prohibit abortions generally (with the exception of saving the woman's life). At any rate, unborn children are not to be considered persons from a constitutional point of view until they are born.

Thus, in the first three months, the Supreme Court recognized no rights to the fetus, but the longer it lives, the greater claim to state protection is accorded to it.

## Are They Reasonable?

The key to understanding the meaning of this decision is found when we ask what happens, in this kind of reasoning, to the constitutional right of a woman to decide about an abortion after the first day of the fourth month. It disappears. It is no longer hers. Why? Because somehow it is decided that with the beginning of the fourth month "potential life is great enough" to limit her freedom. This argument is the old view of "quickening" dressed in new robes of constitutional law. Since most mothers begin to feel some movement about the end of the third month and the beginning of the fourth month, this was considered in the western legal tradition a good point for indicating that the fetus was "alive" and since its presence had been felt, somehow it had to be taken notice of and protected. At a certain "point in time" mothers lose their freedom to freely and unrestrictedly abort and potential babies "can make claims on the protection of the state."

The point is that this is the most unscientific reasoning that can be used. Biologists and geneticists recognize that "studies in embryology and genetics have conclusively proved that the embryo from conception to birth is a living human individual." New techniques are able to diagnose illness in embryos and treatments have been developed to deal with the condition. Scientists know that the newly conceived child is different than the mother's tissue, the father's genetic make up, or anyone else's for that matter. There is just no justification at all for making an arbitrary and totally unscientific decision to determine that the fetus' claim to protection from the state begins at the time when fetal movements are usually felt.

### Orthodox Christian Truth

The Roman Catholic theological tradition has long, involved itself in the dispute regarding when the soul enters the body, and how this takes place, thus giving credence to the "quickening theory." The Orthodox Christian tradition has never done so. In fact, Saint Basil, in his second canon, makes a point in ruling out this kind of discussion, using the then current terms "formed and unformed" regarding the embryo. "A woman who aborts deliberately is liable to judgment as for murder; among us there is no exact definition of that which is formed and that which is unformed."

He goes on to indicate that justice is to be provided for the fetus by this rule, since destruction of the embryo is murder.

Further, Orthodox theology knows of no stopping point in our human development. Passage from the mother's birth canal is no magical "humanizing" event. The church's theology points to the fact that until we fully realize God's presence in our lives we can't realize our full humanity. In fact there is no end to "becoming human"—we keep growing as human beings from "glory to glory."

In the view of the church, our unique existence begins with our conception and our growth begins in our mother's womb. It continues throughout our life: physically, mentally, socially and spiritually. And it ends only when we die. There is no "stopping place" in between. "Quickening," or as it is paraphrased by the Supreme Court majority opinion, "certain points of time," is simply bad reasoning. It is unscientific. And it is not in accordance with Orthodox Christian truth. It is a poorly reasoned decision.

## 37. WHAT ARE JAILS FOR?

A continuing issue in our society is the question of penal reform. Recently, a highly placed public servant summed up the problem by saying that we know that our present system of dealing with lawbreakers is not working. But, he added, "though we know that changes are needed, no one knows what these changes should be." The discussion about penal reform has two points toward which most of the discussion gravitates. The first favors strict, predictable punishment for every offender. The second sees reform of the criminal as the task of the penal system. Each calls upon the Christian faith to support it, and, in fact, finds that support.

## Punishment

The first group sees jails as the means society uses to punish violators of the law. In this view, criminal law exists to punish the criminal in retribution for the harm done to others and to society as a whole. In the Old Testament, this view was dominant, teaching as it did "an eye for an eye, a tooth for a tooth." Once guilt is established, this view holds, it is the buisness of the law to punish the offender for what he or she has done against society.

In the New Testament, much of this feeling is expressed in the teaching about the State in St. Paul's epistle to the Romans. In its 13th chapter there is a discussion in which St. Paul urges his readers to submit themselves to civil authorities who obtain their governing power from God. He continues, saying, "For rulers are not a terror to good conduct, but to bad . . . if you do wrong, be afraid, for he does not bear the sword in vain; he is a servant of God to execute his wrath on the wrongdoer" (Romans 13:3, 4).

The conclusion to this view is evident. Jails exist to enforce retribution and punishment upon the criminal. In addition, long sentences with little recourse to parole keep dangerous people out of society so that they cannot continue to inflict harm on law-abiding citizens.

## Reform

The second view holds that the penal system should emphasize the rehabilitation of the criminal and his or her restoration to society as a useful and productive citizen. Much of the New Testament teaching tends to support this view. The famous story of the woman caught in adultery is one of many examples. According to the Mosaic Law, adulterers were to be stoned to death. Jesus first embarrassed her accusers into leaving by saying: "Let whoever is without sin among you be the first to throw a stone at her." When they left, Jesus said to her, "Go and do not sin again" (John 8:1-11).

The teachings of the Sermon on the Mount seem to point in that same direction. We are to forgive those who do harm to us. Heaven rejoices when one sinner repents. Jesus' whole mission seems to emphasize the guilt for all for sins committed and the need for repentance and a change of life-style for all. The proponents of this view feel that when this Christian message is applied to criminals, the main efforts of the penal system should not be retribution, but rehabilitation. Thus, these people argue that jails exist to help criminals change their way of life, cease criminal activities and return to society as good citizens who will not be offenders against public order, but in fact will contribute to it.

## Perspective in Conflict

Against those who hold to the first view, the others argue that all that severe and long punishment does is to embitter the prisoner, turning him or her into a criminal for life. They point to the great loss of talent and ability, to the huge cost to keep the criminal in prison, to the hard, cold and merciless character of a criminal system run on the basis of retribution.

However, those who argue for rehabilitation are also criticized. This view is called soft and naive. It is argued that if prisons are run on the basis of rehabilitation, all criminals will soon learn that the most that can happen to them is a short and relatively pleasant stay in jail, and that they can return to society to continue their criminal activities. These critics point to the victims and ask why the law-abiding victims should have to put up with such lax law enforcement procedures.

## A Christian Approach

Without question, the issue is a difficult one to resolve for the Christian. For the reasons listed above, it is impossible to accept either view as wholly right or wholly wrong.

The church has a long history of concern with prisoners. There is a passage in the Last Judgment story in the 25th chapter of Matthew which presents Christ as imprisoned. "I was in jail and you visited me," He says to the righteous. But to the unrighteous he says words of condemnation: "I was in jail and you did not come to me . . . for insomuch as you have not done it unto these the least of my brethren, you have not done it unto me."

In a fine study, written in 1969, Father George Kapsanis has dealt with *The Pastoral Care of the Church for the Imprisoned.* For Kapsanis, who documents the long history of the concern of the church for imprisoned persons, the religious motivation for concern is the building up of the prisoner in Christian Faith and life as well as providing comfort and assistance to those imprisoned. This is in harmony with the major thrust of both of the views we have discussed above. It agrees with the view that crime must be punished, while it does everything possible to reform the criminal.

The Christian view clearly holds that crime must be punished, if only to maintain public order and to restrain criminal activity. But it also clearly seeks the return of the criminal to a good, law-abiding life. How is this to be accomplished?

Doubtlessly our criminal system does need reform. Criminals need to be brought to trial more quickly, sentences should be consistently given, and shorter, without wholesale opportunities for parole. The prison experience should be constructive, leading toward rehabilitation. Frequent violators of the law, who prove to be incorrigible, or who are guilty of particularly heinous criminal acts should not be permitted to return to society until serious repentance is evident and the reformation tested. Society must not be moved primarily by vengeance, but by the desire to save all of its citizens from lives of crime and for useful pursuits.

In this view there is respect for law and order as well as concern for the welfare of the imprisoned. Certainly it is easier to say than to do. But Christians will want to be concerned. They will support those efforts which promise that the Christian ideal will be realized. Toward this purpose pastors must include in their concerns the prisons and jails within their parish boundaries. The Orthodox Church in our country ought to make the title of Fr. Kapsanis' book a reality in our church.

## 38. CRIMINAL JUSTICE

Criminal Justice in the United States has become a serious concern for the Church and the nation. Disrespect for the law and the rights of others is widespread, causing an extremely high crime rate in the United States. There is a confusion in the public mind on the purpose of our Criminal Justice system; the extent to which punishment of criminals ought to go; and the question of human rights of victims and criminals in the war on crime. These and many other issues are serious and complex problems which need much study and analysis. However, the Orthodox Church must also note that its own answer to the issues of crime and criminal justice transcend them and seek to focus on those forces which need to be strengthened in this society so as to reduce the incidence of crime itself.

### Long Standing Concern

Concern for issues of crime and criminal justice have always been part of the Orthodox Christian moral and ethical tradition. The New Testament expects believers to be law-abiding citizens (John 8:10-11, Matthew 5:24-25, 1 Peter 2:12-17); calls upon us to recognize lawful civil authority and to obey it (Romans 13:1-7); has examples of concern for due process (John the Baptist—Mark 6:14-29;

Jesus— Luke 22:52-53, John 18:19-24; St. Paul—Acts
18:12-16, 21:12-16, 23:12-26, 30 and generally Luke
12:57-58); and counsels concern for the imprisoned and
punished by the law as a result of the persecution of the
Church. For example, St. John Chrysostom in the 4th century called on rich and poor alike to comfort the imprisoned
materially and spiritually, while sponsoring organized efforts by the Church for the same purpose. The Church
sought, as well, to contribute to the reform of prisoners.
The Greek Archdiocese, in its Clergy-Laity Congresses has
repeatedly addressed the issues of crime, criminal justice
and related issues. (Social and Moral Issues Reports,
Clergy-Laity Congresses, 18—1966; 19th—1980; 20—
1970; 21st—1972; 24th—1978.)

## The Purposes of Criminal Justice

In the public debate, the purpose of our criminal justice
system is at question. Some believe that the purpose is
retribution—that those who do harm to others should
suffer equivalently. Others hold that the purpose is protection of the innocent and law-abiding public from the criminal actions by assuring public order. Still others hold that
the chief purpose is to reform the criminal. Some are very
concerned that the criminal justice system not be used to
suppress minorities and ride roughshod over the rights of
those accused of crimes. At heart, it is hoped that the criminal justice system will deter crime. But nearly all agree,
however, that our present system of criminal justice leaves
much to be desired in its effects on crime, the criminal and
the climate of our society. As a Church we cannot espouse
any one of the above. All have their place in an Orthodox
Christian view of criminal justice. Retribution calls for
fairness and equal treatment; protection and preservation
of public order is an elementary requirement for life; the
reformation of character and life-style is a powerful and
human Christian emphasis; the protection of the weak and

friendless is also an important moral concern of the Church. However, each of these is also subject to serious perversion which causes outrage as well. Retributive punishment easily becomes vengeance and brutality; "law and order" approaches frequently become compassionless, bitter and inflexible; reform approaches may coddle the prisoner, reducing the deterrent effect of the criminal justice system to an absolute minimum; concern for the rights of prisoners may indicate a lack of concern for their victims. The Church knows that every system of criminal justice is imperfect and wishes to work together with all other interested parties in working toward a truly protective, humane, just, and reformative system of dealing with criminals. As a Church, it needs to expand its understanding of the issues and contribute to their solution. As the Orthodox Church, however, our bias will be in the direction of humane treatment leading toward the repentance, reform, and rehabilitation of the criminal.

## Severity of Punishment

How severe should criminal punishment be? Do we support capital punishment? In the first place it needs to be noted that any and all punishment, in order to be effective, needs to be meted out expeditiously and without undue delay. As the 19th Clergy-Laity Congress put it in 1968, "Crime will be reduced when the criminal is convinced that if he commits a crime, his apprehension will be swift, his trial prompt and his sentence substantial." Further, the sentence must be served in surroundings and an environment which will not further criminalize and brutalize the prisoner. Thus, the 21st Clergy-Laity Congress, in 1972 made broad recommendations regarding prison reform, calling for "a greater awareness of the correctional injustice that exists in our society: the need to improve prison facilities, antiquated and overcrowded in most states, to provide appropriate rehabilitation and training programs for inmates, and to urge a general updating of the entire penal system aimed at treating the detained offender humanely."

The issue of capital punishment concerns us, as well. Theoretically, the justification of capital punishment from the point of view of the Old and New Testaments, as well as from the history and practice of the Church throughout history may be argued both pro and con. Objectively, in fact, there has been both strong condemnation of it and tolerance of capital punishment in the history of the Church. However, in our present system of criminal justice it has been manifestly practiced almost exclusively upon minority poor; it is not wise or fair to support it. As a result, our Archdiocese has opposed the practice of capital punishment. But society has to be protected from the incorrigibly violent person. Consequently, a more careful and thoughtful sentencing and parole system needs to be devised— something the Orthodox Church will wish to contribute to in its formation.

## Protecting Human Rights

The protection of human rights has always been a serious concern of the Church. Basic rights are to be protected for all persons, often these claims for human rights will conflict. Certainly, innocent victims of crime should have a priority. As the 19th Clergy-Laity Congress (1968) said, we need to "reestablish a system of social self-protection that is clear, definite, unshakeable . . . one that inspires respect because it works. It means cracking down on those who defy the law not only from the outside, but on officials and judges who weaken and corrupt it from within. It means reasserting authority where authority belongs, instead of artfully remodelling legal concepts to benefit defendants always, the general public, never." Yet, we would never support a movement which would deny fairness, protection under due process, and recognition of human rights to the accused and those convicted of crime, as well. There is need, however, to correct an evident imbalance in the present system that thwarts justice as a result of an exaggerated concern with procedure.

## The Real Solution

In the last analysis, however, the solution to crime will not be found in the criminal justice system. The system deals with the failures of the rest of the structure of society in the formation of human beings who have formed in themselves basic and elementary character traits of decency, honesty, responsibility and respect for law and their fellow human beings. The Church and the school contribute greatly to the formation of this fundamental attitude for social living in the individual when they function properly. But the most profound influence is given by the home. Again and again, our Church has emphasized the crucial importance upon the formation of character by the home. When the home fails, the destructive consequences reach to every segment of society, including—as the most dramatic example—the court of criminal justice and the prison.

Yet even this will not suffice without firm grounding of families and persons in the source of all law, justice, truth and goodness—God. Our Orthodox Church asks, in the words of its 21st Clergy-Laity Congress (1972):

> . . . *ultimately, perennially, and from all ages to all ages, can there be any real freedom, any real order in society and real justice, without the redeeming force and power of our Lord Jesus Christ? We can only be really free if we seek truth in Jesus, whose blood was shed for our redemption. And how can there be justice without love, for God so loved the world that He gave His only begotten son for our salvation. The Lord Jesus is the only present and ultimate answer!*

## 39. WHAT ABOUT CAPITAL PUNISHMENT?

No one who considers the question of capital

punishment with seriousness finds it a simple and easy issue to resolve. Christians find it even more difficult. Our history in dealing with the question of the right of the State to execute offenders against its law is not even. Before trying to arrive at some conclusion, it will do us good to see what we, as Orthodox Christians, had done about it in the past.

### Two Conditions—Two Answers

The early church was opposed to capital punishment. There were several reasons why this was so. The first was based on the teachings of the Lord. Capital punishment is based on the idea of retribution. All systems of law, both ancient and modern, espouse it. The Old Testament expresses this view with the teaching of "an eye for an eye and a tooth for a tooth" (Leviticus 24:20). The conclusion is inevitable: "Whoever strikes a man so that he dies shall be put to death" (Exodus 21:24). Jesus' teaching on retribution is very clear. "You have heard that it was said, 'An eye for an eye and a tooth for a tooth.' But I say to you, do not resist one who is evil . . . love your enemies and pray for those who persecute you." (Matthew 5:38-39, 44).

Later the opposition to retribution was easily applied to capital punishment. The early Christians were frequently victims of this law in the Roman Circus where they were sentenced to die by the judges of the empire. But Christians were also opposed to capital punishment because it was the taking away of a life. The clearest statement of early Christian opposition to capital punishment comes from the pen of Lactantius (240-320):

> *When God prohibits killing, He not only forbids us to commit brigandage, which is not allowed even by the public laws, but He warns us not to do even those things which are regarded as legal among men . . . And so it will not be lawful for a just man . . . to accuse anyone of a capital offence, because it makes no difference whether thou kill with a sword or with a word, since killing itself is forbidden. And so, in this*

*commandment of God, no exception at all ought to be made to the rule that it is always wrong to kill a man, whom God has wished to be regarded as a sacrosanct creature.* Institutes VI, XX, 15.

So long as Christians were themselves persecuted by the State and there was no possibility of Christians holding public office and having to enforce "those things which are regarded as legal among men" the Christian view was relatively easy to maintain. If the State was going to execute men for capital crimes, it was the State's business, but Christians should not have anything to do with it.

The problem arose, however, when after Constantine the Great, Christians began to enter government service and became the makers of the law, the judges and the enforcers of public order and peace. In the words of Saint Paul, the ruler "is God's servant for your good. But if you do wrong, be afraid, for he does not bear the sword in vain. He is the servant of God to execute his wrath on the wrongdoer" (Romans 13:4).

So long as it was considered necessary for the sake of justice, good order and the deterrence of wrongdoing, most Christians found it possible to go along with the idea of capital punishment. It was not seen as an ideal, or as a desirable thing, but as an unfortunate necessary evil. In no case was it ever argued that capital punishment was desirable for itself or that it ever fitted very well with the Christian ideal.

## The Situation Today

With more information available to us today about the consequences of capital punishment, many Christians are of the opinion that it no longer serves as a deterrent to crime. Statistics in the United States show that the existence of capital punishment in some states and its absence in other states seems to have no measurable effect on the rate of various capital crimes.

Perhaps one reason for this is that long ago capital punishment ceased to be uniformly enforced. For a long time now, persons accused of capital crimes who can afford the legal expertise nearly always escape capital punishment. Generally speaking, only the weak, the poor, the friendless have been executed in more recent years in America.

### Some Conclusions

Thus, it appears from a Christian point of view that the State has the right to employ capital punishment as a deterrent to crime, if it chooses. However, if capital punishment is maintained, then it ought to be consistently enforced. It is clear that in America we are not willing to do that. This provides an opportunity for Christians to seek to make their own ethical view into the law of the land. Repealing capital punishment, however, requires that persons who are dangerous to the safety of good citizens and who threaten the order of society either be fully reformed or permanently imprisoned. Abolishment of capital punishment requires a consistent and strong penal policy.

In the light of the above view, the Greek Orthodox Archdiocese was correct in joining with other Christians to urge the abolishment of capital punishment. However, the Archdiocese and all Christains should couple this act with strong efforts in the direction of prison reform.

## 40. ARMS RACE

The Orthodox Church constantly remembers that the Lord Himself is a peacemaker and blesses those who make peace (Matthew 5:9). As a result, the Church as a whole and its ethical teaching is opposed to war, which it sees as a most terrible evil which nations inflict upon each other. In the strict sense of the word, there is no good war. The early

Church strongly condemned war. St. Cyprian's (246 A.D.) denunciation of war is typical when he condemned wars scattered everywhere with the bloody horror of camps. "The world is wet with mutual bloodshed: and homicide is a crime when individuals commit it, but is called a virtue when it is carried on publically. Not the method of innocence, but the magnitude of savagery, procures impunity for crimes." (*To Donatus,* 6, 10).

## A Bias Toward Peace

Yet other moral realities keep the Church from adopting and advocating a pacifist position. Thus, recognition that the innocent need to be defended and human life must be protected, became especially vivid to the Church with the establishment of the Byzantine Empire in 325 A.D., an Orthodox Christian state. The Church then recognized the possibility of just wars of defense and even named as saints some persons who were soldiers or military leaders.

However, none of this changed the essential conviction of the Church that peace is a great good to be prayed for, worked for and sought after with Christian love and diligence. The spirit of the Orthodox Church is captured in this passage from St. John Chrysostom: "If in order to put an end to public wars, and tumults, and battles, the priest is exhorted to offer prayers for kings and governors, much more ought private individuals to do it." He proceeds then to speak of "grievous kinds of war" including . . . "when our soldiers are attacked by foreign armies." He does not mention, however, offensive wars of conquest or retribution (*Homily on Timothy,* Homily VII).

## Recent Positions

In the recent history of the Archdiocese, peace was one of the topics which Archbishop Iakovos raised at the first Clergy-Laity Congress over which he presided (15th Clergy-Laity Congress, 1958) expressing the Church's "determination to fully support the policies of our government for the securing of the peace of the world and justice." This concern found itself expressed again and again in the Clergy-Laity Congresses in subsequent years as we joined the nation in agony over the war in Vietnam. That experience led the Church, in strong calls to "commend every effort and every movement to terminate war and hostility in every area . . . (and) to take seriously the pursuit of peace." (20th Clergy-Laity Congress, p. 69), and "to urge ceaseless activity toward the goal of peace in Vietnam . . . (and) pledge ourselves to labor in all possible ways to bring peace . . . (21st Clergy-Laity Congress, p. 70).

## Horrible Possibilities

As terrible and horrible as that war was, it pales in significance before the possibilities of a nuclear holocaust in our own times. The stockpiled atomic weapons proliferating now not only in Russia and the United States, but also in many of the smaller powers, are only the first of a series of frightening facts which make nuclear war simply unthinkable. The massive arsenals of weapons have created for humanity a peace based on an "overkill" capacity able to destroy the world many times over. It is a peace, but one based on premises, which, should they be violated just once, under any circumstances, whether by design or accident, would prove to be suicidal. Further, our armaments and weapons are not limited to these, as though they are not enough. Sophisticated germ warfare, poison gases, space weapons, electronic devices all promise to destroy whomever and whatever remains after a nuclear holocaust. Even if this "stand-off peace" were to continue indefinitely, it must be criticized on other grounds. Its cost is enormous, depriving humanity of resources which ought to be properly used for more humanitarian needs. It is also capable of accidental or unplanned initiation either through mechanical or human error. Recent malfunctions of our system, based on the failure of a small and inexpensive part show that this is not beyond possibility.

## The Church as Peacemaker

The role of "Peacemaker" for the Church must surely include support for the present policy which seeks bilateral arms reductions. The Strategic Arms Limitation Agreement signed in Moscow in May of 1972 was the beginning of a long series of efforts to reduce the intensity of the arms race, an effort which is now being slowed down because of current attitudes in the USA which sound increasingly militaristic and accepting of the idea of war. As a Church we deplore anything which will further slow the already slow pace toward the reduction of death-dealing armaments. Orthodox Christians understand the need for defense and therefore do not of necessity subscribe to proposals of unilateral disarmament. But certainly it is morally necessary to urge our government to work diligently in furthering a reduction of the potentials for nuclear war.

As a "Peacemaker", our Church will want to help develop understanding and knowledge among the faithful Orthodox Christians entrusted to her pastoral care concerning the grave dangers of war. Further, we ought to expand our understanding of those members of the Orthodox Church who feel that in Christian conscience they cannot bear arms. They should be counseled to assume other forms of service to the people of the nation in accordance to the laws of the land regarding conscientious objection and to accept that others in the Church with equally good conscience will differ with them.

As a "Peacemaker" the Orthodox Church will continue to support all legitimate efforts to reduce international tensions of whatever form. We will recognize that at heart, many of the causes of war are based on the power of sin in humanity, which can be overcome only by increased communion with the God of Peace. We also recognize that a sure encouragement of peace will be to contribute to the alleviation of poverty, social injustice and oppression.

As a "Peacemaker" the Orthodox Church will not only continue to pray in public worship "for the peace of the world," but will encourage all the faithful to make peace a subject of their personal petitions.

Peace is both a gift from God and a human achievement. Orthodox Christians and their Church must be both in word and deed "Peacemakers."

## 41. ECOLOGY: A CHRISTIAN OVERSIGHT?

About a decade or so ago the first "National Environmental Teach-In" was held on American campuses in order to bring to the attention of students, faculty and the general public the problem now known as "ecology."

In a handbook, especially prepared for the day, there was an article which claimed that the Christian teaching about the creation of man and his "dominance" over the natural environment was responsible for the ecological crisis our nation was facing.

The charge was put in quite stark terms:

The book claimed that Christianity, in absolute contrast to ancient paganism and Asia's religions (except, perhaps, Zoroastrianism), not only established a dualism of man and nature but also insisted that it is God's will that man exploit nature for his proper ends . . . By destroying pagan animism, Christianity made it possible to exploit nature in a mood of indifference to the feelings of natural objects.

Because Christianity taught that man was master over his environment; and because Christianity's emphasis of human superiority over the rest of creation led man to study nature (science) and then to control it (technology), "Christianity bears a huge burden of guilt" for the ecological mess in which we find ourselves, according to the "Teach In" authors.

This view has been repeated and refined subsequently so that we now hear quite frequently of an additional attack on the Christian Faith, in addition to so many others: "The Ecological Argument Against Christianity." What do we have to say to it?

## Two Answers

There are two ways of answering that criticism. The first deals with the explicit teaching of the Church about nature. In a recently published Greek Orthodox ethics textbook, the author points to the fact that "the duties of man toward nature are based on the faith that God, who is the creator of nature and everything in it, loves his creation and providentially cares for it." If we are "created in the image of God," then we too must care for nature. "Thus," continues the Orthodox ethics text, "man, imitating God, ought to love nature, and within the limits of his powers, he should care for it." This means that man's dominance over nature permits and requires his knowledge of it (science) as well as his control over it (technology) but not his destruction of it (ecological mismanagement).

This leads to the second answer to the criticism that the Christian Faith is the cause of that mismanagement. Christians are aware that the question of ecology is not unique as a moral issue. Most of us realize that there are many things in life which are good or bad, not in themselves, but in how we choose to handle them. Like sex, money, pride, ambition, etc., man's relationship to nature is a question of how we choose to behave: it is an issue of moral freedom. In religious terms, the careless exploitation of the world which God created, is sin. Christianity cannot and does not teach that we should sin.

The misuse of power and responsibility does not mean that authority and responsibility should not exist. Rather, it means that man should exercise his duties responsibly and avoid irresponsibility. It means, in regarding the environment, that man should wisely manage and direct God's gift to him, not exploit and ravage it. There is ecological sin; and modern industrial, technological men commit it every day. But it is erroneous to charge that Christianity teaches men to do it.

### Orthodoxy's Record

There is another observation to be made. Orthodox Christianity's record on the ecological question is generally recongized to be very much better than that of Western Christianity. The "Teach-In" article mentioned above recognized that truth quite explicitly.

The key to the contrast may perhaps be found in a difference in the tonality of piety and thought which students of comparative theology find between the Greek and Latin churches.

According to this author, the Orthodox Church saw nature within the framework of spiritual illumination, contemplation and a "symbolic system, through which God speaks to men," a view which is "essentially artistic." For the Western Christian tradition, knowledge about nature (science) was knowledge about God, the manipulation of nature (technology) was an expression of man's superiority over God!

The author should have realized, if he understood the Orthodox teaching about God as compared to that of the Western Church, that there is no connection between knowing the essence of God and knowledge of His creation.

If there is any connection between Christian theological teaching and ecological sin, it will not be found in the theology of the Orthodox Church!

## 42. THE ETHICS OF THE ENERGY CRISIS

One of the casualities of living in an affluent society was

the virtue of frugality, or temperance. Throughout the church's age-long teaching of how people should behave, there was a thread of consistent teaching which instructed the faithful not to be constantly trying to get more things, and to conserve those things which one had.

## Get More, Spend More

With the coming of the affluent society and the emphasis on an ever larger Gross National Product, frugality and the temperate use of this world's goods was downplayed. In fact, when you think about it, it was almost turned into a vice. Not so many years ago, young people were reported to actually be laughing at elders who spoke of "saving for a rainy day." The "get more, spend more" mentality had made a shambles of the old ethical ideals of frugality and temperance in reference to the material things of life.

Well, we are beginning to have second thoughts. We are hearing not only of gasoline, heating fuel and crude oil crises, but rumors of other crises also pervade the atmosphere. Will there be enough bread all summer? Both rumors and the facts of shortages, as well as the messages of the persistent environmentalists, make the convincing affirmation that the age of wanton affluence is over.

## Old-Fashioned Virtues

Suddenly, what was recently an old-fashioned, out of date virtue has been refurbished! Conserve! Don't waste! Limit and restrict your demands and requirements! All these are the signs of the times. The message has come through to us all, and as a consequence we have changed our behavior. Lights go out where they once burned profligately. Car pools are established where once "going out for a ride" was a standard way to entertain the family. What used to be called frugality or temperate living is now "ecological awareness" and "conservation virtues."

## Wrong Reasons—Right Reasons

However, there is still a difference. The motivating force behind this change of behavior, and the rehabilitation of the virtues of frugal and temperate use of material goods is economic necessity. Christian values see the whole issue in a quite different light. God is the creator. Humans use the creation for purposes which are pleasing to God. One of those purposes is to meet our own basic needs: food, shelter, health, education, etc. Surplus of goods over those basic needs is not ours to waste, to use for personal pleasure or to commit to purposes of prideful prestige. In the spirit of the Parable of the Talents, the Parable of Lazarus and the story of the Good Samaritan, we are stewards of God's blessings to us in the service of our neighbor.

For Christians to waste resources, to spend time and effort on personal indulgence beyond the point of necessary recreation, is to deny food to the hungry, shelter to the homeless and medication to the sick. The Christian ethos thus sees frugality and temperate living as an exercise of Christian "agape" for both God and our fellow man.

The Parable of the Last Judgment tells of two kinds of Christians: one who did works of mercy to the hungry, homeless, sick and imprisoned brother and another sort of Christian who ignored him. To the latter, Jesus said "inasmuch as you did not do it unto these, the least of my brethren, you did not do it unto me!" The Christian motive for the conservation of resources is that it provides resources for Christian love. Frugality and temperate living are virtuous because they provide the means for Christian concern for our neighbor's welfare.

## Autarkeia

In Greek, the word for frugality and temperate living is "autarkeia." It literally means "to be satisfied with what you have." There is a sense of that virtue which we twentieth century Christians must re-learn. It has a sense which is inspired not by economic necessity, nor by the oil shortage, nor by the energy crisis. Rather, as we face the newly revived demands of our time for frugal and temperate use of our nation's and the world's resources, let us do it, inspired by the fundamental motive of all Christian action: "Let all you do be done in love" (1 Corinthians 16:14).

## 43. DEATH AND DYING

Something significant is happening regarding the attitudes of people toward death and dying. It represents a major change in the way our civilization has regarded death in the past. Certainly, not all persons have adopted this new view, but it is having important implications for some of the major issues in our technoligical age: abortion, the meaning of human life, euthanasia, atomic warfare and hunger.

### The Traditional View

The traditional view in Western Civilization is that death is an enemy, an evil which is resented, fought against and battled, even though it is seen as inevitable. Death is darkness. It is the end of life on earth as we know it. It is the conclusion of our efforts, our hopes, our dreams, our expectations, our existence as earth-borne beings. That is why, considered in itself, death is evil. The Fourth Horseman of the Apocalypse is a powerful biblical symbol of the evil of death.

> *"And I saw, and behold, a pale horse, and its rider's name was Death, and Hades followed him; and they were given power over a fourth of the earth, to kill with a sword and with famine and with pestilence and by wild beasts of the earth" (Revelation 6:8).*

That is why St. Paul could write, without threat of opposition, that "the last enemy to be destroyed is death" (1 Cor. 15:26).

But death is one thing and dying is another. In the experience of dying, dying is conceived as a different kind of process, depending on the overall view of life which we may have. In history, dying and its meaning are conditioned by the way we respond to the fact of death. It was Freud who said, "The goal of all life is death."

There are three basic responses to death which have served to dictate how we die. The first is fear. This is the view which dominates the thinking about dying in history. Death is recognized as the end, the tragedy that it is, and people approach the end with the agony of self-extinction. Thay battle it with a fierce clinging to life, in spite of its unavoidability.

The second basic response to death belonged in the past to a small group of philosophers. Epicurus rationalized death out of existence: "Thus that which is the most awful of evils, death, is nothing to us, since when we exist, there is no death, and when there is death, we do not exist."

The philosopher and essayist Montaigne continued this tradition of whistling in the dark by saying it even more sharply. "Of all the benefits which virtue confers upon us, the contempt of death is one of the greatest." Contempt for death makes dying appear easier. For then it is as if it is nothing—not enemy, not tragedy, not pain, not suffering. Consequently, it is a non-thing which is neither to be feared, respected, nor regarded.

### The Orthodox Response

The third basic response is the Christian response. Orthodox Christianity—unlike Western Christianity—does not view physical death as a natural result of living. Rather, because death is the consequence of humanity's sin, it is not natural to us. For Orthodoxy, death in its ultimate sense is a perversion of our nature: it is a destructive extension of sin in our lives. "Therefore, as sin came into the world through one man, and death through sin, and so

168

death spread to all men because all men sinned. . ." (Romans 5:12).

Yet, Christians hold also that the power of death over us has been destroyed, essentially, by the saving work of Jesus Christ. Thus, even though death continues to be evil, dying takes on new meaning. The Christian no longer fears dying, even though death is a fearsome thing. He knows and trusts in "our Saviour, Christ Jesus, who abolished death and brought life and immortality to light through the gospel" (1 Timothy 1:10). Together with Saint Paul, every Christian facing his or her own death can repeat the words of the Prophet Isaiah, "Death is swallowed up in victory," as well as the words of Prophet Hosea, "O death, where is they victory? O death, where is thy sting?" (1 Corinthians 15:55-56). The Christian knows the evil and the tragedy of death, but meets and overcomes it through sharing in the resurrected Christ's victory over death.

### The "New" Error

The "new" error about death and dying is the popularization of the ancient philosophers' disregard for death. In past days, the reality of death was felt and experienced by people directly. People died at home, in the circle of the family. Their bodies were "laid out" in the living room. Burial was real and the phrase "earth to earth and dust to dust," punctuated by shovelfuls of soil falling upon a wooden casket, made the tragedy and finality of death a truth vivid in the minds of all.

Today's practices—lonely hospital deaths, chemical embalming, "double-lined metal caskets, with deluxe concrete water-resistant concrete vaults," closed-casket funerals and other such "distance-makers"—camouflage the tragedy and evil of death in our experience.

Death becomes distant. Dying, too, is becoming distant. The elderly are shunted out of our lives. Dying hospital patients are never allowed to speak of their impending death. If it takes too long, it is now the fashion to encourage it along (euthanasia). On the other end of the scale, if the death of a fetus can be hidden from public view, we can pretend that no death has really occurred, and thus encourage it for purposes of convenience (abortion).

The callousness toward death which characterizes the dictator-politician (Joseph Stalin: "A single death is a tragedy, a million deaths is a statistic") and the military man (General William Sherman: "I begin to regard the death and mangling of a couple thousand men as a small affair. . .") now pervades our whole nation in the face of the death by starvation of hundreds of thousands of people in various nations of the world. All of this occurs while the great nations inch toward the regulation of atomic warfare, hardly moved by the contemplation of the deaths of millions upon millions of people in a nuclear holocaust.

### Time for a Change

The consequences of this trivilization of death are already upon us. The future will intensify them unless we change our minds, recognizing the stark significance of death, and the power of Christ which gives us victory over death. A well known ethicist of our day, Prof. Paul Ramsey of Princeton University, wrote an article entitled "The indignity of 'death with dignity.' " In his concluding statement he writes:

> ". . . if the 'bodily life' is neither an ornament nor a drag but a part of man's very nature; and if the 'personal life' of an individual in his unique life-span is accorded unrepeatable, noninterchangeable value—then it is that Death the Enemy again comes into view. Conquered or Unconquerable. A true humanism and the dread of death seem to be dependent variables." (Hastings Center Studies, May 1974, Vol. 2, No. 2)

If that is a true statement, and from an Orthodox Christian point of view it encapsules great truth, it provides great resources for some deep and profound Christian thinking about death. Death as enemy, as evil, as tragedy takes its last pound of flesh and attacks the very meaning of life when it is perceived to be "unconquered" or "unconquerable" in fact. Only when we can sing in faith the glorious dismissal hymn of the Resurrection at our Orthodox Christian Easter services is death seen as "conquered." Only then is dying a victory and openness to life.

> *"Christ is risen from the dead;*
> *By His Death,*
> *Death destroying.*
> *And to those in the Tombs*
> *He giveth life."*

## 44. THE RIGHT TO DIE

Recently, newspapers throughout the country published a story illustrated by a photograph of a crying mother. An insert in the photograph pictured a smiling, happy boy. The caption read as follows:

> *A Mother Mourns—Anna Mair clutches photograph of her son, David, after she orders doctors to turn off respirator which had kept the 10-year-old Denver boy alive since he was struck by a car . . . Mrs. Mair made the decision after officials at St. Anthony's Hospital told her David's brain had died. Youngster was buried earlier this week. (UPI).*

The increasing sophistication of medical technology will make such situations more and more common. Orthodox Christians, with strong desires to "do what is right" need to have some clear ideas regarding such issues so that they may be prepared to face them in the future. Some of us have already had to face such decisions.

### Orthodox Guidelines
Our Orthodox Christian tradition on this issue does not

provide us with specific guidance. How could it, since the medical techniques which make the issue possible, are so new? Yet, our faith provides us with certain basic guidelines with which we are able to make the difficult decisions when necessary. We have several basic ethical traditions in Orthodoxy upon which we are able to draw.

The first is that God is the author of life and that we have the responsibility to defend, protect and enhance life as a basis for living God's will. God is the giver of life, and "in his hand is the life of every living thing and the breath of all mankind" (Job 12:10). To wrongfully take the life of an innocent person is murder and is condemned as a sin (Exodus 20:13).

On the other hand, "it is appointed for men to die once" (Hebrew 9:27). Physical death is inevitable, yet it is something which comes normally *in spite* of our efforts to preserve life. There is something which rings of the barbaric in calls for the "elimination" of human life. That is why *the Orthodox Church completely and unalterably opposes euthanasia.* It is a fearful and dangerous "playing at God" by fallible human beings.

But modern medicine has perhaps gone to the other extreme. It is able now to "preserve" lives which God struggles to take! The various substitute organs devised by medical science are good and useful as therapeutic means. When, for instance, an artificial lung or an artificial kidney is used during an operation, it permits treatment of the diseased natural organ by the surgeon. Often these artificial mechanical organs are used over a period of time so that the patient's life is maintained while the weakened organism is allowed time and energy to recuperate. Sometimes, such as with kidney machines and artificial lungs, almost permanent use of the machine is required. In all these cases, life is enhanced and preserved. Normally speaking, the use of such methods is a necessary and useful step in the therapeutic process whose goal is the restoration of health and life.

## A Time To Die

However, sometimes it occurs that the body's functions break down so completely and irrevocably that these machines literally keep a dead body functioning as if it were alive! The Church holds that there comes a time to die for each of us. In fact, there is a service in the prayer book for this specific situation. When ordinary medical efforts are incapable of sustaining life, and when the body literally struggles to die, the Church prays as follows:

> . . . *Thou has commanded the dissolution of the indescribable bond of soul and body, O God of Spirits, and has ordered them to be separated by Thy divine will. The body is thus to be returned to the elements from which it was made, and the soul is to proceed to the source of its existence, until the resurrection of all. For this reason we implore Thee, the eternal and immortal Father, the Only-begotten Son and the All-Holy Spirit, that Thou bring about the peaceful separation of the soul of Thy servant (name) from his/her body.*

Here is a specific and unique situation when the church prays that life might come to an end. The implications of this view are clear for the kind of situation which Anna Mair faced. Clear Orthodox Christian guidelines in these cases are available to us:

1) We have the responsibility, as a trust from God, to maintain, preserve and protect our own lives and those lives entrusted to us;

2) In case of illness, we are obligated to use every method available to us to restore health, both spiritual and medical;

3) Life is so precious and to be so respected that even when health cannot be fully restored, it should be protected and maintained;

4) When, however, the major physical systems have broken down, and there does not seem to be any reasonable expectation that they can be restored, Orthodox Christians

may properly allow extraordinary mechanical devices to be removed. When the body is struggling to die, when its numerous physical systems break down, when it cannot be reasonably expected that the bodily systems will be able to regain their potential for life, the Orthodox Christian is no longer obligated to continue the use of extraordinary mechanical devices;

5) The decision should never be taken alone. It should be shared by the family, if possible. And, certainly, it should be made on the basis of expert medical opinion in consultation with the physician in charge of the case. It should also be made with the advice, counsel and prayer of the priest.

This action should never be confused with euthanasia, which brings to an end, deliberately and consciously, a life which is capable of maintaining itself with normal care. It is one thing to kill and murder; it is quite another to "allow the peaceful separation of soul and body."

## 45. EUTHANASIA

Does an individual ever have the "right to die?" Must life be prolonged when there is little or no chance of its restoration to "meaningful existence?" Is there any moral justification for curtailing the life of a terminally-ill patient in order to free him from unbearable suffering? These questions, punctuated by the much-publicized and controversial Karen Ann Quinlan case, are becoming increasingly important as we strive to enhance not only the quantity but the quality of human life. They concern a very real problem faced by our own Orthodox Christian clergy and laity alike in dealing with acutely and terminally-ill patients. We therefore ask, "What is the stance of the Orthodox Church concerning mercy-killing or euthanasia?" And "to what extent are we the faithful enjoined to maintain human life?"

The Orthodox Church has always taught that euthanasia constitutes the deliberate taking of human life, and as such is to be condemned as murder. Yet, rapid advances in modern technology and new means of maintaining life have created a need for an explanation and clarification of this position.

## The New Situation

Euthanasia (Greek for "good death") is defined as "the act or practice of painlessly putting to death persons suffering from incurable and distressing disease." But the use of modern medical equipment and methods of treatment often leads to a prolongation of the dying of a terminally-ill patient and not to the recovery of his or her health. We must therefore consider whether the deliberate withholding of such "extraordinary measures" is morally equivalent to euthanasia and, thus, to murder.

## The Old Situation

A partial answer to this question is to be found in the Orthodox perspective of death. The fathers tell us that death is an unnatural wrenching of the soul from the body leading to the destruction of the psycho-somatic unity that constitutes the human person. Here man is a microcosm, uniting in himself the material and spiritual realms of God's creation. In addition, he bears the imprint of image and likeness to God, and in this resemblance, Adam, the first man, enjoyed immortality. But through the Fall man rejected God, the only source of authentic life, destroying the likeness and fracturing the image. He strove to make his own life apart from God and, thus, chose death.

Nevertheless, God did not desire that His creation remain in its fallen state, and in His great mercy, He sent His beloved Son into the world to transform and unite all things in Himself. By His Life, Death, and Resurrection, Christ Jesus restored the image and likeness in man to its original wholeness. All aspects of human existence were thereby transformed including death which through the Resurrection has become a passage into eternal life.

As a consequence, Christians should cherish their life on this earth as a most precious gift from God entrusted to them for a time, never forgetting that this life has been bought with a price and already been made new in Christ. At the same time, we must accept the inevitability of our physical death, not in despair, but with anticipation of that Last Day when we shall all be raised up in a transfigured flesh.

A further inference from this conception of life and death is that we do not deliberately contribute to the death of others. Therefore, euthanasia being a deliberate taking of human life, does not constitute a viable alternative for the Orthodox physician or patient.

## Some Guidelines

While the Church suffers with those who are in grave distress, she cannot so betray her commitment to the preservation of human life. Yet, the Church is not insensitive to the needs of those who suffer and in its concern stresses the Christian obligation to relieve pain and make the patient as comfortable as possible. The use of pain killers, such as morphine, is permissible; where they may constitute an undefined effect on the length of the patient's life, no serious attention need be given, when the motive is the comfort and over-all well-being of the patient.

Those experiencing great physical pain are also reminded that even suffering has acquired new meaning by our Lord's own passion and has become a means to an enhanced communion with God and an opportunity for spiritual growth.

At the same time, the Orthodox Church parts with those members of the medical profession and others who refuse to acknowledge the inevitability of physical death and advocate the use of "extraordinary measures", at whatever material and psychological cost, to keep a patient alive when there is no hope of restoration to a meaningful; functional existence. The Church which prays for the "quick and painless death" (Prayer for the Separation of Soul and Body) of the terminally-ill patient, considers this kind of treatment not only a poor use of scarce medical resources, but a denial of the will of God.

We must remember, of course, that there are no final, clear-cut answers: today's "extraordinary measures" fast become tomorrow's regular life-saving procedures. And any life-death decisions to withold treatment must be considered on an individual case by case basis in consultation with the patient or his next of kin, his physician and spiritual advisor.

## An Important Distinction
The Church, therefore, distinguishes between euthanasia and the withholding of extraordinary means to prolong life unable to sustain itself. It affirms the sanctity of human life and man's God-given responsibility to preserve life. But it rejects an attitude which disregards the inevitability of physical death. The only "good death" for the Orthodox Christian is the peaceful acceptance of the end of his or her earthly life with faith and trust in God and the promise of the Resurrection.

## 46. THE DONATION OF ORGANS

Rapid advances in modern medicine have opened up vast new vistas in an effort to prolong human life and eradicate disease. Most dramatic of these breakthroughs is the transplantation of vital organs from one person to another. Organ transplants are such a new phenomenom that they raise unique and never before encountered theological and ethical questions for our Orthodox faithful: Can we violate the bodily integrity of one person, in order to help another? Can we allow the deliberate "dismemberment" of a lifeless body or the "mutilation" of one living person for the sake of another? Or shall we permit an otherwise healthy person to die when an organ transplant can restore him to a fairly normal and reasonably extended life? In seeking answers to these very complex questions, we turn, as the Church has always done in every dilemma, to that rich and timeless store of Orthodox tradition which continues to serve as a guide in our fast-changing world.

### Sanctity of the Body

Before delving further into the question of organ transplants, it is important to stress that special sanctity accorded our limited bodily existence in the Orthodox Christian faith. The Church affirms that every man and woman is a psychosomatic unity, a union of body and soul, and cannot exist as a human person in permanent separation from his or her physical manifestation in the flesh. As Christians, we recognize as well that our bodies have been sanctified by God's own assumption of human flesh in the incarnation of our Lord and Savior Jesus Christ. And in the glorious light of His Resurrection, we await the resurrection of our own transfigured bodies to new, eternal life. Furthermore, we are reminded that our bodies have become "temples of the Holy Spirit" through our baptism.

From all this, it is apparent that we ought to treat our bodies with reverence as an inseparable part of our very being. We manifest ourselves through our bodies, and therefore ought not to abuse them or violate their integrity and wholeness without good cause.

### A Moral Conflict?

At the same time, we proclaim the free and unselfish love of God Himself called agape to be the highest good of the

Christian life. We accept the call to follow our Lord's example of free self-giving to the fullest—even to the point of giving up our own life for the life of another.

Now the fundamental moral conflict involved in the question of organ transplantation is that between the reverence we hold for our own bodies as "temples of the living God" and our Lord's commandment to love one another even as He loved us—between the duty to preserve the wholeness and integrity of our bodies and the call to sacrifice a part of ourselves for the good of another. There are no absolute answers, but we can offer the following guidelines for Orthodox Christians faced with the decision to donate or not to donate their bodily organs after death.

## Suggested Guidelines

We should probably regard the donation of a duplicated organ, such as a kidney, by a living person to save the life of another person as a loving act of mercy. The donor is to be commended if he perceives his sacrifice not as a violation of his bodily integrity, but as a gracious and loving unselfish gift of himself.

The Church does, however, place a limit on the generosity of its members. Orthodox are not enjoined and even prohibited from giving to the point of suicide. The donation of such vital, unduplicated organs as the heart or liver by living persons is out of the question, nor is the donation of duplicated organs condoned when there is reasonable doubt that the health of the donor can be maintained by the sole remaining organ of the pair.

In addition, the Church recognizes the highly personal nature of the decision to donate. For this reason, it does not condemn the potential donor who shies away because of a particularly strong aversion to the mutilation of his own flesh; that decision too is a natural and healthy one and may be guided by Divine Providence to some future need. Furthermore, we are aware that every individual possesses his own unique calling and gifts and will respond to the gospel message accordingly. In making any decision, the potential donor must be careful to weigh all the factors entering into his decision, and examine both his motives and the resulting consequences. Does he choose not to donate out of selfishness or dislike for the dying person, or out of a genuine and healthy regard for self? Or does he give not out of love and compassion for his brother, but out of an externally-imposed shame and guilt? No one should feel compelled to donate, and no person should donate if there is no reasonable chance that such a sacrifice will restore the patient to health.

## Organ Donation After Death

The donation of cadaver organs present additional and overlapping questions. The Orthodox Church maintains that such a donation must remain a free and unconstrained gift of self. It would in all likelihood oppose any legislation which would make the routine salvaging of usable organs standard procedure in hospitals, unless prior objection has been registered. Even in death, the human body retains its sanctity. It is horrifying to think that our bodies might become part of a giant "rummage sale", a collection of "exchangeable parts", that one goes to the hospital to obtain, just as one goes to an automobile "graveyard" to find spare parts for his car. And it is essential that the wishes of a person who explicitly expresses the desire that his body be buried fully intact be respected. Neither should vital organs be taken from the corpse of any person who has expressed no opinion on the matter if his surviving relatives find the trauma of partial dismemberment too much to bear in their grief.

On the other hand, if a person believes his organs ought to be donated for the benefit of others and expresses his desire either in his will or through provision of the Uniform Anatomical Gift Act, or lacking explicit direction, his surviving loved ones find such a donation consonant with the major thrust of his life, then the Orthodox Church in all likelihood would offer no objection to the act.

**Other Issues**

But it is never considered moral to hasten the death of a potential donor for the sake of salvaging vital organs. Here we encounter such technical medical questions as to what constitutes death: whether death occurs with the disappearance of a heart beat or the halting of brain wave patterns.

It is also imperative to enquire whether the candidate for an organ transplant is obligated to accept the donation. His/her decision should be based on a consideration of other alternatives, the existence of a reasonable chance of success, and the threat to health of a living donor. In some cases, the recipient may sense a threat to his own bodily integrity by the intrusion of another's organ; we ought not condemn any person who refuses a transplant for this reason.

Special caution must be exercised in regard to heart transplants. As yet, a high degree of success has not been demonstrated in this area, and the risks most often outweigh the benefits of this procedure. Here the Church also wishes to guard the special place given the heart in Orthodox tradition as the seat of the emotions or the soul. Yet, it is not relevant for these ethical questions to locate the soul in any specific place, such as the heart.

In conclusion, the donation or reception of organs is a personal decision which must be made on an individual basis in light of the teachings of the Church. Such decisions should be made in an attitude of prayerful faith and in consultation with physician and spiritual advisor.

## 47. CREMATION

The current wave of criticism directed against the unethical practices of some avaricious funeral consultants, the appearance of such prepaid funeral programs as the Purple Cross Plan, along with the sky-rocketing cost of dying, is leading an increasing number of Americans into accepting the responsibility of preplanning and meeting the expenses for their own funerals—and many are choosing cremation over the traditional, more expensive form of burial.

## Traditional Attitudes

The Eastern Orthodox Church has traditionally never accepted cremation as a legitimate means of disposing of dead bodies, and the increased prevalence of this practice in contemporary American society raises new questions for its faithful. Is cremation acceptable as a means of combatting escalating funeral expenses? Can it be justified as a necessary method of saving space in already overcrowded cemeteries? What value should we place on the remains of our limited physical existence? It is hoped that the answers set forth in this chapter will explain and clarify the position of our Church and settle any confusion created by this issue.

While utilized in some cultures for centuries, cremation was not widely practiced in the Christian world until our own era; and it is worthy to note that its use is common where religion seeks escape from bodily existence. It was only natural that the early Christians would carry on the Jewish practice of burying their dead. Opposed to cremation, burial was definitely better expressive of the Christian feeling of reverence for the human body and more consistent with the expectation of the Resurrection of the Dead in Christ. This reverence stemmed from the awareness of man as a unity of body and soul—of man as a microcosm, the crowning of God's creation, uniting in himself the material and spiritual realms. Revered was the fleshly part of man's nature, stamped with the imprint of God's own image and likeness, and assumed and sanctified by the Son of God, our Lord and Savior Jesus Christ Himself.

### Cremation as a Symbol of Unbelief

With the dawn of the Age of Enlightenment in the eighteenth century came a transfer of faith in God to the power and mind of man. In a climate of anti-clericalism and doubt, cremation became both an effective means of defying the Church and denying the bodily resurrection of the dead. Cremation thus became the ultimate expression of a belief in the complete annihilation of every human person in physical death. Under these circumstances, the Church, out of pastoral concern for maintaining the true faith of the flock, believed it wise to adopt a stance counter to the practice. And although cremation is no longer widely practiced as a renunciation of God and as a denial of the Resurrection, the Church seeks to continue to safeguard from future intrusions, the same fundamental truths of our Christian faith.

### The Arguments

Acceptance of cremation would represent a radical departure from an established practice for which there seems to be no adequate reason to institute a change. The argument that cemeteries waste space does not stand in a nation as immense as our own, especially when the universality of modern transportation makes burial sites away from urban centers easily accessible. The sky-rocketing cost of dying is not seen at this time as a compelling reason to sanction cremation. For the Church does not ask that funerals be extravagant and costly, but that a certain amount of respect be maintained for the human body that was once the temple of a human soul.

Thus, although there is no compelling theological reason for opposing cremation in an absolute sense, the Church, nevertheless, due to a pastoral concern for the preservation of right beliefs and right practice within the Tradition of the Fathers, and out of a sense of reverence for its departed, generally feels obligated to continue its opposition to this practice. Those who insist on their own cremation, therefore, will not be permitted a funeral in the Church (Although a memorial service may be chanted over the body at a funeral home). The only exception occurs when the Church is confronted with state law prohibiting burial and insistent on cremation, as in the situation in Japan, or in the case of some natural disaster where cremation is necessary to guard the health of the living. In these special situations, the Church allows cremation of Orthodox people by "economia."

### Gravest Concern

Of greatest concern to the Church is the total disregard for the sanctity of the human body and the denial of the possibility of an afterlife implied by cremation. We ask, are our bodies of such little worth that we might as well reduce them to ashes? We must not forget the example of St. Spyridon, St. Gerasimos, and St. Nectarios, whose bodies remain uncorrupted to this day as a witness to the Resurrection to new life on the Last Day. These saints were so sanctified and transfigured by the Holy Spirit dwelling within them that their bodies also bear the marks of holiness and serve as a source of sanctification and healing power for believers even today.

As Orthodox, we believe that the relics of all the saints and the bodies of every Orthodox Christian are to be revered as temples of the Holy Spirit. We know, as well, that all human flesh has been redeemed and sanctified by God's own assumption of a body in Christ Jesus. In addition, all Orthodox are enjoined to commemorate and pray for the dead. And what better expression of this spirit can be found than in visits to the gravesites of departed loved ones?

One the other hand, the Church does not teach that the body must by necessity remain completely intact in anticipation of the Day of Resurrection. To believe so would be to limit the power of God. We also have the example of countless martyr-saints burned at the stake—we cannot by any means admit that they will lack their bodies on the Last Day.

For all these reasons the Orthodox Church does not approve the practice of cremation.

# Epilogue

Each day the communications media bring to our attention new and difficult problems. It is never easy to deal with these issues. As we have seen, however, our Orthodox Christian faith does not stand silent. It can deal with many of these concerns in a forthright and serious fashion. At the heart of the Orthodox Christian response to contemporary issues is the doctrinal, spiritual and liturgical life of the Faith.

Whoever seeks to deal with the myriad of contemporary issues, will find in Orthodox Christianity a firm foundation to direct his thoughts and judgments. Yet, even with the sure foundation of the Orthodox Faith, it must be pointed out that our conclusions are subject to critique.

The truth of Orthodoxy on any issue is subject to the "conscience of the Church." Rather than a final answer, these responses in many cases, merely introduce the subject to treatment from an Orthodox Christian point of view.

This book has seriously sought to articulate in these pages what might be the Orthodox Christian point of view on each of the issues treated. Yet, hierarchs, priests and laypeople will do well to examine the points of view expressed here with an Orthodox Christian conscience, thus contributing to the formation of a firm Orthodox Christian position on many of the topics discussed. The Orthodox Church is a living and vital church. This volume seeks to be both an expression of that truth and a challenge to it as well.